Public Policy Evaluation

Evaluation
Approaches and Methods

David Nachmias

THE UNIVERSITY OF WISCONSIN—MILWAUKEE

Public Policy Evaluation

Approaches and Methods

ST. MARTIN'S PRESS · NEW YORK

Library of Congress Catalog Card Number: 78-71818
Copyright © 1979 by St. Martin's Press, Inc.
All Rights Reserved.
Manufactured in the United States of America.
32109
fedcba
For information, write St. Martin's Press, Inc.,
175 Fifth Avenue, New York, N. Y. 10010

Cover design: Joseph Notovitz

cloth ISBN: 0-312-65561-4
paper ISBN: 0-312-65562-2

ACKNOWLEDGMENTS

Figure 3.7: Donald T. Campbell: From "Reforms as Experiments," *American Psychologist*, 24 (April 1969), 413 and 419. Copyright 1969 by the American Psychological Association. Reprinted by permission.

Figure 3.8: Franklin E. Zimring: From "Firearms and Federal Law: The Gun Control Act of 1968," *The Journal of Legal Studies*, 4 (1975), 177. Copyright by the University of Chicago Law School. Reprinted by permission.

Table 4.3: Jules J. Wanderer: From "An Index of Riot Severity and Some Correlates," *American Journal of Sociology*, 74 (March 1969), 503. Copyright 1969 by the University of Chicago Press. Reprinted by permission.

Figures 6.10 and 6.11: Gary L. Tompkins: From "A Causal Model of State Welfare Expenditures," *Journal of Politics*, 37 (May 1975), 406 and 409. Copyright 1975 by the *Journal of Politics*. Reprinted by permission.

Appendix A: Harold O. Rugg: From *Statistical Methods Applied to Education* (Boston: Houghton Mifflin, 1917). Reprinted by permission of Houghton Mifflin Company.

Appendix B: R. A. Fisher and F. Yates: The Table is taken from Fisher and Yates: *Statistical Tables for Biological, Agricultural and Medical Research*, published by Longman Group Ltd., London (previously published by Oliver and Boyd, Edinburgh), and by permission of the authors and publishers.

TO MY PARENTS

Preface

This book is concerned with both the theory and methodology of public policy evaluation. It attempts to analyze and compare various conceptual models on which evaluations can be based and to explain the statistical techniques most useful in evaluation research. My central intention is not so much to break new ground as to foster systematic thinking in an emerging scientific discipline.

It is my contention that the idea of causality lies at the heart of all policy evaluation. Accordingly, the book is organized around the central issues involved in drawing causal inferences. The first three chapters concentrate on the construction of theoretical models of cause-and-effect relationships and the development of research designs to test such models. The last three chapters discuss the data-analysis techniques—such as linear, curvilinear, and multiple regression; time series; and recursive and nonrecursive structural equation models—that can be used to test the adequacy of evaluation models.

My literary debts are testified to in the bibliography. Less obvious are the contributions of friends and colleagues whose assistance has been more personal. Without involving them in any way in failures on my part, I would like to express my gratitude to Michael Baer, Ann Lennarson Greer, Scott Greer, Ronald D. Hedlund, John D. Montgomery, and David H. Rosenbloom. I wish also to thank N. Joseph Cayer, Frank Swant, and Michael J. White for their valuable comments on the manuscript at various stages of development. Gary T. Henry and Louise A. Miller performed many tedious tasks while retaining their good humor.

I am grateful to the Literary Executor of the late Sir Ronald A. Fisher, F.R.S., to Dr. Frank Yates, F.R.S., and to Longman Group Ltd., London, for permission to reprint Table III from their book *Statistical Tables for Biological, Agricultural and Medical Research*. (6th edition, 1974.)

At St. Martin's Press, Glenn Cowley started me on the project, and Thomas Broadbent and Bertrand Lummus helped me bring it to completion. The assistance of the editorial staff, in particular Glorya Cohen and Carolyn Eggleston, has been invaluable.

Special thanks go to my wife, Chava, who is my source of expert counsel and sound advice.

D. N.

Contents

One
Policy Evaluation for What?   **1**
A Performance Perspective   1
A Framework for Evaluation   6
Stages of Evaluation Research   12

Two
Policy Experimentation   **21**
Assessing Effectiveness:
    The Classic Experimental Design   21
Controlled Experimentation   29
Types of Experiments   35

Three
Quasi-Experimental Evaluations   **47**
Pre-Experimental Designs   47
Quasi-Experimental Designs   51

Four
Measurement and Social Indicators   **74**
Sources of Data   74
Social Indicators   80
Measurement Scales   84
Construction of Measures   88
Validity and Reliability   100

Five
Regression as a Data-Analysis System   **111**
Linear Regression   111
Curvilinear Regression   124

Multiple Regression   129
Time-Series Analysis   134

Six
Structural Equation Models   145
Structural Models   145
Recursive Models   146
Nonrecursive Models   156

APPENDIX A: THE STANDARD NORMAL DISTRIBUTION   173
APPENDIX B: THE *t* DISTRIBUTION   174

A SELECTED BIBLIOGRAPHY   175

INDEX   189

Public Policy Evaluation

Approaches and Methods

Chapter One
Policy Evaluation for What?

Although the government has in recent years devoted a growing share of the nation's resources to policies and public programs for meeting societal needs, dissatisfaction with these programs has never been more widespread: complaints about inefficiency, ineffectiveness, and waste are increasing; voters are more and more often rejecting the proposals of their elected officials. In education, for example, William Gorham has observed that from 1963 to 1970 the percentage of school bond issues approved by voters declined from 72 percent to 53 percent in spite of the efforts of school officials to put fewer issues on the ballot (only 1,216 in 1970, compared with 2,048 in 1963).[1] Other manifestations of discontent have taken the form of cynicism, alienation, protest, and occasionally violence.

A PERFORMANCE PERSPECTIVE

Dissatisfaction with the results of public policies is widespread not only among beneficiaries of the policies but also among those responsible for delivery. One government official diagnosed the situation as follows: ". . . the federal government has developed two defects that are central to its existence: (a) it does not know how to tell whether many of the things it does are worth doing at all, and (b) whenever it does decide something is worth doing, it does not know how to create and carry out a program capable of achieving the results it seeks."[2] More systematic documentation of this state of ignorance was provided in a study funded by the Department of Housing and Urban Development and conducted in close cooperation with the Executive Office of the President. The authors of the study concluded:

> The most impressive finding about the evaluation of social programs in the federal government is that substantial work in this field has been almost nonexistent. Few significant studies have been under-taken. Most of those carried out have been poorly conceived. Many small studies around the country have been carried out with such lack of uniformity of design and objective that the results rarely are comparable or responsive to the questions facing policy makers. There is nothing akin to a comprehensive federal evaluation system. Even within agencies, orderly and integrated evaluation operations have not been established.[3]

Today, more legislators, government officials, and members of the academic community are committed to systematic research on problems of public policy effectiveness to improve the basis on which policy makers can exercise their judgment. The more frequent use of the term "evaluation research" best reflects this commitment. In the early 1970s, about two hundred new evaluation studies were begun each year with direct federal support and with average budgets of about $100,000 each. By now, the number of policy and program evaluation studies started each year has probably doubled, and the costs have risen markedly.[4] Another measure of this commitment is that federal and state legislation involving public programs increasingly refers to formal evaluation in the text of an act or in pending bills. Before discussing in greater detail the objectives and the methodology advanced in this book for evaluation research, it is necessary to draw a distinction between policy outputs and policy impacts.

Outputs Versus Impacts

A prevailing myth among many laypersons is that once the government sets its mind to do something and allocates sufficient funds, its goals will be achieved—at least in great part. The myth persists even though experience with policies and programs such as urban renewal, community action, public housing, and equality of educational opportunity has shown that this is not the case. One major reason for this myth is failure to distinguish "policy output" from "policy impact."

Policy outputs are tangible and symbolic manifestations of public policy; they are observable indicators of what governments in fact do. Thus, the number of bills passed by Congress and the amount of money spent on urban renewal are policy outputs. As governments change, so do their priorities; as new societal problems emerge, demands for different policy outputs are articulated, only some of which are responded to by decision makers. Obviously, then, policy outputs and description and analysis of how they are determined have been major preoccupations of policy-oriented social scientists.

Policy outputs, however, tell little if anything about performance. The amount of money spent, the units of services provided, the number of cases handled, the number of staff employed by delivery agencies are valid measures of policy outputs, but they do not indicate whether or to what extent the desired objectives have been achieved. *Policy impact*, therefore, refers to performance, that is, the extent to which a policy output has accomplished its stipulated goals. As Thomas R. Dye has pointed out, "No longer do we assume that once we pass a law, establish a bureaucracy, and spend money, . . . the purpose of these acts will be achieved and the results will be what we expected them to be."[5]

Evaluation and Public Policy

The observation that policy outputs do not necessarily accomplish their intended objectives and that at times they may even produce unintended consequences is by no means novel. The process of making judgments of worth is universal: "It is basic to almost all forms of social behavior, whether that of a single individual or a complex organization."[6] However, the methods for making such judgments are numerous and diverse, including conventional wisdom, intuition, and reliance on authorities. Such methods may sometimes lead to correct conclusions, but often they lead to erroneous ones. One method that can reduce the number of erroneous decisions is the formal scientific approach to knowledge.

Viewed from the scientific perspective, policy evaluation research is the objective, systematic, empirical examination of the effects ongoing policies and public programs have on their targets in terms of the goals they are meant to achieve. In this sense, policy evaluation research is goal-oriented research focusing on effectiveness rather than on the decision-making processes that lead to the adoption of policies. Yet, evaluation research may improve the quality of policy decisions if it becomes an integral component of public policy making. With systematic, empirical, objective information on the impact of policies, better decisions can be reached: ineffective programs can be abandoned or radically modified, effective programs can be expanded, and more responsible budget allocations can be made. From this broader perspective, policy impact evaluations "characterize the aggregate flow of decision according to policy objectives of the body politic, and identify those who are causally or formally responsible for successes or failures."[7]

Policy evaluation research, like other scientific research, is neither all powerful nor all weak because it is carried out within a political-bureaucratic context. Some observers take the position that political realities inevitably dominate the extent to which evaluation evidence influences and will affect public policy making: "Evaluations can influence fine-grain program decisions, and that's about it. For any of the big policy decisions, research is marginal. These yea/nay decisions are made on the basis of political tea leaves."[8] Indeed, evaluation evidence is only one source of information that decision makers take into account when adopting policies and public programs. Other factors—political values and ideologies, party loyalties, vested interests—play as significant a role with some decision makers as objective and systematic evidence. Thus it cannot be expected that the findings of evaluation research will be incorporated into the decision-making process in all cases. Evaluation information has to compete with everything else in the policy-making process. Nevertheless, as Carol H. Weiss has observed:

> [Decision makers] are not monoliths . . . As time goes on, if confirming evidence piles up year after year on the failures of old approaches, if mounting data suggest new modes of intervention, this will percolate through the concerned publics. When the political

climate veers toward the search for new initiatives, or if sudden crises arise and there is a scramble for effective policy mechanisms, some empirically grounded guidelines will be available.[9]

Types of Evaluation Research

With the growth of policy evaluation research activities, two distinct but interrelated types of evaluation have emerged: (1) process evaluation and (2) impact evaluation.[10] *Process evaluation* is concerned with the extent to which a particular policy or program is implemented according to its stated guidelines. The content of a particular public policy and its impact on those affected may be substantially modified, elaborated, or even negated during its implementation. Obviously, it is futile to be concerned with the impact of a particular policy if it has not been implemented. For example, in 1967 President Lyndon B. Johnson proclaimed a new program known as New Towns In-Town to create model communities on surplus federal land in metropolitan areas. The objectives of the program were to demonstrate the government's commitment to helping troubled cities, to build new housing for the poor, and to show that much can be accomplished by combining zeal with the resourcefulness and imaginativeness of urban planners. After four years no new towns had been started.[11] So critical and complex are policy implementation problems that Eugene Bardach has conjectured that the "character and degree of many implementation problems are inherently unpredictable. Even the most robust policy—one that is well designed to survive the implementation process—will tend to go awry."[12]

The second type of evaluation research, *impact evaluation*, is concerned with examining the extent to which a policy causes a change in the intended direction. It calls for delineation of operationally defined policy goals, specification of criteria of success, and measurement of progress toward the goals.

Ideally, policy evaluation research should include both a process and an impact evaluation. Howard E. Freeman proposed the term "comprehensive evaluation" for such research endeavors: "A comprehensive evaluation is defined as one in which appropriate techniques and ideas have been brought to bear so that it is possible (1) to determine whether or not a program, intervention or treatment is carried out as planned, and (2) to assess whether or not the program resulted in changes or modifications consistent with the intended outcomes."[13] Such comprehensive evaluations, when feasible, could best serve the attentive publics and decision makers. At present the major concern of evaluation research is with impact evaluation, although even this somewhat restricted concern is in the process of developing.

A FRAMEWORK FOR EVALUATION

Scientific disciplines are formed around a set of questions or problems, viable and testable theories, and rigorous and systematic methodologies. Whereas impact evaluation research has formed its basic set of questions, there is no theory of evaluation per se nor one methodology for evaluation. Most policies and programs to be evaluated are grounded, often implicitly, on the established body of interdisciplinary knowledge. Yet few if any evaluation studies include presentation of the theory or theories involved in the selection of variables of which the relations are investigated. Queries such as why a particular policy is expected to accomplish its goals are generally not articulated. Obviously, if there are no solid theoretical grounds for expecting that a particular policy will accomplish its goals, one should not be too surprised if in fact the policy does not accomplish them.

Relatedly, many evaluation studies use the various and diverse methodologies available to social scientists without critically assessing their suitability to impact evaluation. Such practices not only hinder the progress of policy evaluation as a scientific discipline but diminish the potential for incorporating evaluation findings into the public policy-making process. Among the reasons why the federal government is not making more effective use of evaluation evidence, Pamela Horst and her coauthors point out the following methodological problems: (1) different evaluations of the same policy or program are not comparable; (2) evaluation studies have failed to provide an accumulating, accurate body of evidence; and (3) evaluation studies often address unanswerable questions and produce inconclusive results.[14] A methodology that can effectively tackle such problems of theory and methods is briefly advanced in the following sections of this chapter and elaborated throughout this book.

Causal Inferences

At the heart of all policy evaluation research activities is the idea of causality; that is, a policy is expected to produce a change in the target population in the direction and of the magnitude intended by the policy makers. However, an observation that when program *A* is implemented, goal *B* is accomplished does not necessarily mean that a cause-and-effect relationship exists. As Hubert M. Blalock has observed, "If X is a cause of Y, we have in mind that a change in X produces a change in Y and not merely that a change in X is followed by or associated with a change in Y."[15]

Consider, for instance, crime-control policies. A major objective of such policies is to deter crime. Deterrence, in turn, is viewed as the prevention of behavior that can be said to have had a realistic potential of actualization. Now, does the observation that a person does not commit a crime imply that he or she has been effectively deterred from doing so by a government program? Obviously, the answer depends on whether the individual was inclined to engage in criminal behavior. Furthermore, even if the person was inclined to commit a crime, was he or she deterred by the possibility of apprehension and punishment or by other factors such as the lack of opportunity or peer group influence? Accordingly, even if researchers observe that with the enactment of more aggressive crime-control policies the frequency of actually committed crimes declines, they cannot safely conclude that the two are causally related.

The major problem with establishing causal relationships is that causality belongs to the theoretical domain and consequently cause-and-effect relationships cannot be observed: "One *thinks* in terms of a theoretical language that contains notions such as causes, forces, systems, and properties. But one's *tests* are made in terms of covariation, operations and pointer readings."[16]

Recent methodological developments in the social sciences have been directed toward bridging this gap. An early influential contributor to these developments is Herbert Simon, who suggested restricting the notion of causality to simplified models that are subject to few limitations and that would apply to the real world.[17] The researcher starts with a finite number of specified variables and constructs an explicit model from which testable hypotheses can be deduced. If the model proves inadequate after testing, additional variables can be introduced or the model can be modified. Underlying this process must be the understanding that "there is nothing absolute about any particular model, nor is it true that if two models make use of different variables, either one or the other must in some sense be 'wrong.' "[18]

Having selected a number of variables, the researcher can construct either a deterministic or a stochastic model. A deterministic model is one in which it is postulated that if X causes Y, and if all other causes of Y are held constant (or controlled for), the manipulation of X should result in changes in Y that are completely prescribed by the model. That is, there should be no errors involved in predicting the values of Y when manipulating the values of X. Operationally, this amounts to being able to formulate a mathematical function of some sort. For example, a function such as $y = f(x)$ means that the values of y depend completely upon the values of x, so that for every value of x there is a corresponding value of y. Further, the value of $f(x)$ when $x = a$ is denoted by $f(a)$; a can be a numerical value. To find $f(a)$, merely substitute a for x in the formula for $f(x)$. Thus, if

$$f(x) = 2x^2 - 4x + 2, \text{ then}$$

$$f(a) = 2a^2 - 4a + 2$$

$$f(2) = 2(4) - 4(2) + 2 = 8 - 8 + 2 = 2$$

$$f(3) = 2(9) - 4(3) + 2 = 18 - 12 + 2 = 8$$

and so on.

Even with simplified models of reality, it is rarely possible to construct deterministic models. Variables might have been omitted due to lack of knowledge, or the measurement of variables in the model might be inaccurate. This necessitates the introduction of error terms into the equations. Unlike deterministic models, stochastic models include error terms, thus allowing for variation that is not caused by the variables in the model, as well as estimation of measurement errors. The mathematical function is replaced in stochastic models by the regression equation.

Having selected a causal model, the researcher proceeds in two directions. Employing the causal assumptions, he or she attempts to deduce certain predictions that can be translated into testable hypotheses. Simultaneously, operational procedures that can be applied to test the hypotheses are being formulated: "Our ideal in the first instance is some sort of deductive system of reasoning; in the second, it is the perfect experiment."[19] In practice, however, deviations from both deductive systems of reasoning and perfect experimentation occur. Purely deductive systems of reasoning are difficult to apply in view of the present state of knowledge. In many cases the researcher must lean on controversial assumptions (e.g., policy makers are completely rational) and/or inductive reasoning. We will discuss policy experimentation and problems associated with experimentation in the real world in chapter two.

Impact Models

The notions of causality, modeling reality, and testing the models to infer cause-and-effect relationships can be applied for the purposes of evaluation research through impact models and rigorous and systematic methods for testing such models. Models in general are fundamental to public policy research. In fact, E. S. Quade maintains:

> Decision-making itself is a process of sequential model use. Decision-makers constantly shift from noncalculated or unconsciously calculated decisions to explicitly calculated decisions, that is to say, from calculations based on primitive intuitive or tacit models to occasional calculations based on sophisticated models . . . There is no such thing as not using a model in analyzing a decision.[20]

Essentially, a model is an abstraction of some part of the real world. It is a representation of reality that is adequate for the problem of concern. Models are made up of variables that are relevant to the problem of concern and the relations among these variables. "We ask questions of the model and from the answers we hope to get some clues to guide us in dealing with the part of the real world to which the model corresponds."[21] Inevitably, models simplify reality, but such simplifications are often necessary for understanding it. Three major steps are involved in constructing models: (1) delineation of the variables that are relevant to the problem under study, (2) explication of the significant relationships among the variables, and (3) formulation of propositions regarding the nature of these relationships. Relationships can be expressed in mathematical form and then subjected to quantitative empirical analyses.

Impact models can serve evaluation research in a manner similar to the ways in which models serve the analysis of public decisions. An impact model translates theoretical ideas about the modification of behavior and/or societal conditions into a set of variables relevant to the policy under evaluation and into a number of concrete propositions pertaining to the relationships among these variables. Both action and research can be based upon such impact models. More explicitly, an impact model consists of input statements, one or more propositions concerning the changes that the input (policy or program) is expected to produce and how the changes will affect the behavior or the conditions intended to be modified.[22]

For example, decision makers might have reached the conclusion that there is insufficient utilization of public transportation in big cities. The objective of their program might be a substantial increase in such use, and they may develop a program based on economic incentives as a means for accomplishing the objective. Even if the program does not explicitly state so, decision makers are presuming that a program based on economic incentives will cause changes in people's behavior. Furthermore, they are assuming that their program will produce the desired changes in behavior and that these changes will lead to a greater utilization of public transportation. The decision makers are also probably supposing that a greater utilization of public transportation will reduce pollution, conserve energy, and reduce traffic congestion. In this example the impact model consists of three propositions:

1. The program of economic incentives will induce changes in attitudes toward utilization of public transportation.
2. Changes in attitudes will produce changes in behavior.
3. All other things being equal, changes in behavior will increase utilization of public transportation.

The general form of impact models is illustrated in Figure 1.1.

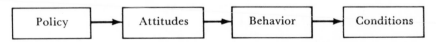

Figure 1.1   **General Form of Impact Models**

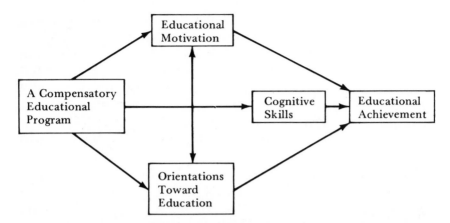

Figure 1.2 **Arrow Diagram Specifying the Expected Relationships
Between a Compensatory Educational Program and
Educational Achievement**

Further elaborations of impact models consist of attempts to
delineate the concrete variables involved; to outline the boundaries
within which the variables operate (the target population); to specify the time lag between implementation of the policy and manifestations of its effects; and to formulate the theoretically expected
relationships among the variables—direct versus indirect causal
variables, and recursive or nonrecursive relationships.*

For example, an impact model specifying how a compensatory
educational program consisting of intensive tutoring and extracur-
ricular activities (the program variables) is expected to improve the
educational achievement of underprivileged children (the target
population) is illustrated in Figure 1.2, where the arrows stand for
the hypothesized causal relations. The goal of the program is to
produce a positive change in the level of educational achievement.
This, however, is a complex process. At least three critical variables
affect the educational achievement of children: general attitudes
toward education, educational motivation, and cognitive skills. Positive orientations toward education directly increase educational
achievement, as do educational motivation and the level and type

---

* A recursive relation is one in which a change in one variable produces a change in
another variable, but not vice versa. A nonrecursive relation represents two-way causation.

of cognitive skills. Positive orientations toward education also increase educational achievement indirectly via educational motivation and vice versa. Thus, the impact model has to specify the expected relations between the compensatory educational program (and, more specifically, the program variables) and the critical intervening factors. In our example, the program is expected to enhance educational achievement through its impact on educational motivation, orientations toward education, and cognitive skills.

Howard E. Freeman and Clarence C. Sherwood observe that at present such fully explicit impact models are rare:

> Too often, impact models consist of nothing more than the implicit assumptions which underly the program's operation. These assumptions may have been drawn from previous studies, undertaken on small samples or in other locales—or they may have little or no empirical base at all, being drawn from the untested ways in which practitioners have performed in the past. [The absence of explicitly formulated impact models, in turn] prevents replication of the program, and severely limits the opportunities for controlling its quality and evaluating its effectiveness . . . there is no basis for understanding why it [the program] worked or for reproducing it and its effects on a broader scale and in other communities.[23]

Because of the absence of a theory of evaluation per se, explicit impact models should serve as the workhorses of policy evaluation research.

STAGES OF EVALUATION RESEARCH

Policy evaluation research, like all scientific research, should be a constant and continuous process. In this process six distinct but interrelated research operations can be identified:

1. Identification of goals
2. Construction of a causal impact model
3. Development of an appropriate research design
4. Measurement and standardization
5. Data collection
6. Data analysis and interpretation

Goal Identification

In basic research the investigator begins with a problem of his or her choice. Next, based on a theory or theories, one or more variables to be explained (dependent variables) are selected, and hypotheses about the variables that are expected to explain or predict (independent variables) the dependent variables are generated. In evaluation research the process is often reversed: "One begins with an independent variable—the program—and is asked to assess how it affects a set of only vaguely identified goals."[24]

When the goals of a policy or a program are ambiguous, diffuse, or diverse, assessment of the extent to which they have been achieved becomes a formidable task. For example, much of the controversy over the Head Start program has surrounded its objectives. The program's proclaimed goals were to compensate the alleged educational disadvantages suffered by poor children which hindered their educational achievement when they entered regular school programs. One evaluation (the Westinghouse study) showed that Head Start children were not appreciably helped in cognitive and affective skills.[25] Critics of the evaluation study charged in turn that such a finding is beside the point because there are other important goals, such as improving the children's physical conditions, that the program might achieve.

The goals set for the Community Action Program further illustrate the difficulties involved in the very early stages of policy evaluation research. Title II of the Economic Opportunity Act defined a community action program as one:

> (1) which mobilizes and utilizes resources, public or private, of any urban or rural, or combined urban and rural, geographical area (referred to in this part as a "community"), including but not limited to multicity unit in an attack on poverty; (2) which provides services, assistance, and other activities of sufficient scope and size to give promise of progress toward elimination of poverty or cause or causes of poverty through developing employment opportunities, improving human performance, motivation, and productivity, or bettering the condition under which people live, learn, and work; (3) which is developed, conducted, and administered with the maximum feasible participation of residents of the areas and members of the groups served; and (4) which is conducted, administered, or coordinated by public or private nonprofit agency (other than a political party), or a combination thereof.[26]

Not all policies and public programs are subject to the same degree of ambiguity in the setting of goals. The goal of manpower retraining programs, for instance, is to impart marketable occupational skills, and their effectiveness can be assessed by the extent to which they manage to do so. Indeed, there might be some disagreement over what occupational skills are and which ones are more marketable, but unless participants in the program are able to function better in the job market, the program is ineffective.

In general, however, the problems of public policy are likely to be "squishy" problems;[27] that is, they may have no definite formulation and no rule of thumb to tell the researcher when he or she has a solution. Furthermore, the style of public decision making, in which bargaining, negotiation, give-and-take, and compromise are common for reaching mutually acceptable policy outputs, contributes to the emergence and the existence of ambiguous, hazy, and difficult-to-identify policy goals. Yet, if a policy's objectives cannot be stated clearly, specifically, and in measurable terms, there is no point in pursuing a scientific impact evaluation study.

Several procedures and considerations are helpful when attempting to identify a program's goals. First, it is useful to distinguish among immediate, intermediate, and ultimate goals. Immediate goals are the anticipated results of "the specific [program] with which one is momentarily concerned,"[28] such as the establishment of a community center in a crime-prone neighborhood; intermediate goals "push ahead toward the accomplishment of the [ultimate goal],"[29] such as the actual activities of individuals in the center; the ultimate goal refers to the effect of achieving the intermediate goal upon the amount of crime in the community. Ultimate goals thus are the final anticipated consequences of policies and programs.

Second, the program's personnel are to be consulted and asked to specify its goals. In some cases, however, the personnel will not reach a consensus and will not articulate propositions that provide an adequate basis for evaluation research. For example, with respect to the Affirmative Action program in the federal bureaucracy, David H. Rosenbloom found that "Neither the Civil Service Commission's Office of Federal Equal Employment Opportunity nor the EEO staffs in agency headquarters necessarily know what goals, if any, have been set."[30] In such cases one can "read everything about the program . . . talk to practitioners at length, observe the program in operation, and then sit down and frame the statement of goals himself."[31] Two major problems may evolve from such an indirect procedure. One is that the researcher "may read his own professional preconceptions into the program and subtly shift the goals (and the ensuing study) in the direction of his own interests."[32] The other problem is that when the research is completed, the decision makers and the program personnel may dismiss the findings, arguing that they had been trying to accomplish different goals.

A third procedure, and perhaps the most useful for identifying goals, is for the researcher to collaborate with the program initiators and personnel in the very early stage of the program. Conferring with the program people, the researcher can suggest successive approximations to the goal statements, the program staff can modify them, and discussion can continue until agreement is reached. The Delphi technique is one formal way to operationalize this process.

Essentially, Delphi is an iterative procedure for eliciting and refining the opinions of a group of individuals by means of a series of questionnaires. The group consists of experts, policy makers, and responsible program practitioners. The idea is to reach an agreement and to improve the decision-making process by subjecting the views of the individual participants to one another's criticism in ways that avoid the psychological drawbacks associated with unstructured face-to-face exchanges. Identity of the participants may be concealed until the end of the scenario. Information is exchanged among the participants by the researcher. After each questionnaire the information generated in previous stages is fed back to the participants so that they can use it to revise their earlier answers. The group judgment is measured by a statistical index, usually the median. This way of defining the group response reduces pressures for conformity and ensures that the opinion of every group member plays a role in determining the final response.[33]

Construction of an Impact Model

Having identified the goals of a policy, the researcher can proceed to construct an impact model, the empirical analyses of which can provide evidence of the extent to which the policy has accomplished its goals. The attributes of impact models were specified in the previous section. Here it should be added that conferring with decision makers and program personnel before, during,' and after construction of the impact model is useful for a number of reasons. First, the chain of reasoning that led the decision makers to choose a particular policy may be better appreciated. Second, the courses of action taken by the program personnel have in many cases to be incorporated into the impact model. In the process of implementation, program personnel might encounter unanticipated problems of such significance that the impact model would have to be modified to include them as critical variables. Impact models represent certain aspects of reality; the more accurate the representation, the more effective the impact model for purposes of evaluation.

Last, if decision makers and program personnel are consulted, there is a higher probability that the study findings will affect future decisions concerning the policy or program. To be incorporated into the decision-making process, evaluation findings must be adequately communicated to decision makers and program implementers. Such findings can be more effectively communicated if the overall framework of the evaluation study is understood and agreed upon.

Development of a Research Design

Once the impact model is developed, the researcher is confronted with the task of structuring the process of collecting, measuring, analyzing, and interpreting data. This is the aim of a research design. A research design is a logical model of proof that guides the investigator in the various stages of the research.

Earlier it was argued that when feasible impact models and hypotheses deduced from them are to be tested experimentally; all other things being equal, the "perfect experiment" permits the most valid assessment of the causal relationship between a policy and its goals. (The perfect experiment as a model of proof is discussed in chapter two.) Not all policies and programs, however, are amenable to experimentation. Social, political, and ethical considerations may prevent experimentation. This, in turn, calls for the construction of alternative research designs. These are generally referred to as "quasi-experimental" designs. (The logic of their construction and the major features of the more commonly employed quasi-experimental designs are discussed in chapter three.) It should be stressed that all these alternative designs take the perfect experiment as their ideal; the perfect experiment represents a model from which all adaptations are derived.

Measurement and Standardization

A policy's goals are to be expressed in measurable terms. Measurements that focus on immediate and intermediate goals are especially significant when evaluation results are needed before the ultimate goal is to be realized. Moreover, once the goals are identified and the impact model constructed, some measurable standards must be set to determine how much progress toward the goals has been achieved. In other words, it is essential in policy evaluation research to measure the impact of policies and the relationships among the variables in the impact model. A detailed discussion of measurement, measures construction, and the validity and reliability of measures is presented in chapter four. Here, the rather recent notion of input measurement will be introduced.

Just as policy impacts vary, so do program variables. For example, in manpower retraining programs some participants attend every session whereas others attend irregularly; some participants receive more attention from the instructors than others do. Participants also vary by sex, age, race or ethnicity, socioeconomic background, and many other important variables. Further, variations are found among program personnel, length of service, location, auspices, management, and implementation. All these lead to program variations. Measurement of such variations is important because it fills in the "details of what the general program description has outlined."[34] That is, such measurements clarify the meaning of the program in a real environment. Furthermore, the measurement of policy or program variables contributes to a more discriminating understanding of the working of each component; it becomes possible to assess the effects of each program component on the target population (see chapter three).

Data Collection

Data for evaluation research can be obtained from numerous sources and through various methods. The more commonly used sources and methods are described in chapter four. There is no one source nor one method that exclusively suits evaluation research. To a large extent decisions about the kinds of data to be collected are governed by the nature of the policy to be evaluated, the kinds of variables included in the impact model, and the research design. Furthermore, there is no one source of data nor one method of collection that does not have some inherent limitations. The researcher should be aware of the advantages as well as the problems involved in employing any kind of data and any data-collection method.

Data Analysis and Interpretation

Decisions about the kinds of data-analysis techniques to use are governed in social science research as much by convention as by considerations of research design. Whereas analysis of variance, for instance, is the workhorse of psychologists, correlational methods predominate in sociological and political science research. For policy evaluation research, where the concern is over notions of change, prediction, and causality, we believe that regression analysis is a suitable and effective technique. The logic and mechanics of simple linear, nonlinear, and multiple regression analysis are the focus of chapter five.

The regression model is also the major technique for testing impact models in which some of the policy variables (or independent variables) would not only bring about a change in the target variable (or dependent variable) but would also affect other policy variables, as exemplified in Figure 1.2. Chapter six deals with structural equation systems that permit the testing of these more complicated but nevertheless more realistic impact models.

Interpretation of the findings in view of the impact model and the goals set for the policy conclude one cycle of the research process. If the study is well executed, it will provide systematic and empirical evidence of the extent to which the policy has accomplished its goals. Such evidence will, of course, have to compete with a host of other factors that decision makers take into consideration in the process of making public policy decisions.

NOTES

1. William Gorham, "Ignorance Is Blissless for Government," in *Improving Management for More Effective Government, 50th Anniversary Lectures, 1921– 1971* (Washington, D.C.: General Accounting Office, 1972).

2. Jack W. Carlson, "Can We Do Anything Right?" *Washington Monthly*, 1 (November 1969), 75.
3. Joseph S. Wholey et al., *Federal Evaluation Policy*, 4th printing (Washington, D.C.: Urban Institute, 1975), p. 15.
4. Howard E. Freeman, "The Present Status of Evaluation Research," in Marcia Guttentag, ed., *Evaluation Studies: Review Annual*, II (Beverly Hills, Calif.: Sage, 1977), p. 19.
5. Thomas R. Dye, *Policy Analysis: What Governments Do, Why They Do It, and What Difference It Makes* (University, Ala.: University of Alabama Press, 1976), p. 95.
6. Edward A. Suchman, *Evaluative Research* (New York: Russell Sage Foundation, 1967), p. 7.
7. Harold D. Lasswell, *A Pre-View of Policy Sciences* (New York: Elsevier, 1971), p. 29.
8. Quoted in Lois-ellin Datta, "The Impact of the Westinghouse/Ohio Evaluation on the Development of Project Head Start," in Clark C. Abt, ed., *The Evaluation of Social Programs* (Beverly Hills, Calif.: Sage, 1976), p. 174.
9. Carol H. Weiss, "Evaluation Research in the Political Context," in Elmer L. Struening and Marcia Guttentag, eds., *Handbook of Evaluation Research*, I (Beverly Hills, Calif.: Sage, 1975), p. 24.
10. See, for example, Howard E. Freeman and Clarence C. Sherwood, *Social Research and Social Policy* (Englewood Cliffs, N.J.: Prentice-Hall, 1970), pp. 11–15.
11. Martha Derthick, *New Towns In-Town* (Washington, D.C.: Urban Institute, 1972).
12. Eugene Bardach, *The Implementation Game: What Happens After a Bill Becomes a Law* (Cambridge, Mass.: M.I.T. Press, 1977), p. 5.
13. Howard E. Freeman, "Evaluation Research and Public Policies," in Gene M. Lyons, ed., *Social Research and Public Policies*. The Public Affairs Center, Dartmouth College (Hanover, N.H.: University Press of New England, 1975), p. 146.
14. Pamela Horst et al., "Program Management and the Federal Evaluator," *Public Administration Review*, 34 (July/August 1974), 301.
15. Hubert M. Blalock, Jr., *Causal Inferences in Nonexperimental Research* (Chapel Hill: University of North Carolina Press, 1964), p. 9.
16. Ibid., p. 5.
17. Herbert Simon, *Models of Man* (New York: Wiley, 1957), pp. 10–13.
18. Blalock, *Causal Inferences*, p. 15.
19. Ibid., p. 20.
20. E. S. Quade, *Analysis for Public Decisions* (New York: Elsevier, 1975), p. 141.
21. Ibid.
22. Freeman and Sherwood, *Social Research and Social Policy*, pp. 7–9.
23. Ibid., p. 8.
24. Ilene N. Bernstein, "Validity Issues in Evaluative Research: An Overview," in Ilene N. Bernstein, ed., *Validity Issues in Evaluative Research*, Sage Con-

temporary Social Science Issues, XXIII (Beverly Hills, Calif.: Sage, 1976), p. 8.

25. Robert L. Granger et al., *The Impact of Head Start: An Evaluation of the Effects of Head Start on Children's Cognitive and Affective Development,* I (Westinghouse Learning Corporation and Ohio University, June 1969), p. 8.

26. Economic Opportunity Act of 1964, 78 Stat. 508, Title II, Sec. 202(a).

27. This term was introduced by Ralph E. Strauch in "A Critical Assessment of Quantitative Methodology as a Policy Analysis Tool," P–5282 (Santa Monica, Calif.: Rand Corporation, 1974).

28. Suchman, *Evaluative Research,* p. 51.

29. Ibid.

30. David H. Rosenbloom, "Implementing Equal Employment Opportunity Goals and Timetables in Federal Service," *Midwest Review of Public Administration,* 9 (April–July 1975), 108.

31. Carol H. Weiss, *Evaluation Research* (Englewood Cliffs, N.J.: Prentice-Hall, 1972), p. 28.

32. Ibid.

33. For a more comprehensive presentation of the Delphi method, see Norman C. Dalkey et al., *Studies in the Quality of Life: Delphi and Decision-Making* (Lexington, Mass.: Lexington Books, 1972); and Juri Pill, "The Delphi Method: Substance, Context, a Critique and an Annotated Bibliography," *Socio-Economic Planning Sciences,* 5 (February 1971), 57–71.

34. Weiss, *Evaluation Research,* p. 46.

Chapter Two
Policy Experimentation

I mpact models are conceptual frameworks pertaining to the hypothesized causal relations between a policy and its stipulated goals. Causal inferences cannot rest on anecdotal or circumstantial evidence; they must be grounded on high-quality data that rigorously and systematically link the policy variables to the target variables. A research design is the scheme that guides the process of collecting, analyzing, and interpreting data. It is a logical model of proof that allows the making of valid causal inferences. The following section explicates the logical structure of research designs. Next, the various factors that might invalidate causal inferences are discussed. The last two sections focus on policy experimentation in contrived and natural environments.

ASSESSING EFFECTIVENESS: THE CLASSIC EXPERIMENTAL DESIGN

The classic research design for assessing the extent to which policies and programs are effective consists of two comparable groups: an experimental group and a comparison group. These two groups are equivalent in many ways but differ in some, most notably that the experimental group is introduced to a policy or a public program and the comparison group is not. To evaluate the effectiveness of a program, measurements on the target variables, designated scores, are taken twice from each group. One measurement, the *preprogram* score, is taken prior to the introduction of the policy in the experimental group; a second measurement, the *postprogram*, is taken after exposure to the policy has taken place. The difference between the postprogram and the preprogram scores is compared in each of the two groups. If the difference is significantly large in the hypothesized direction, the researcher can infer that the policy is effective.

This research design can be illustrated as in Table 2.1, where X symbolizes the policy; O_i the measurements on the target variable; and d_e and d_c the differences between the postprogram and preprogram measurements in each group.

The Manhattan Bail Project initiated by the Vera Institute in New York City applied such a design.[1] The Vera Institute sought to furnish criminal court judges with evidence that many persons could be safely released prior to trial and without bail if reliable information concerning defendants' backgrounds were available to the court at the time of bail determination. The target population included persons accused of felonies as well as misdemeanors; individuals charged with very serious crimes were excluded from the experiment. New York University law students and Vera staff reviewed the defendants' records of employment, families, residences, references, current charges, and previous records to decide whether a pretrial release without bail should be recommended to the court. The total group of recommendees was split randomly into experimental and comparison groups, and recommendations were made to the judge only for persons in the experimental group. The target variables were pretrial releases granted, case dispositions, sentences, and default rate.

Judges in the first year granted parole to 59 percent of the recommended defendants, compared with only 16 percent in the comparison group; recommendations based on information, then, served to increase the rate of release without bail. Sixty percent of

Table 2.1   **The Classic Experimental Design**

	Preprogram		Postprogram	Difference
Experimental group	O_1	X	O_2	$O_2 - O_1 = d_e$
Comparison group	O_3		O_4	$O_4 - O_3 = d_c$

the recommended group was either acquitted or had their cases dismissed, compared with 23 percent of the comparison group. During 1961–1964, less than 1 percent of the experimental group failed to show up in court for trial—a rate considerably lower than that for similarly charged defendants who had posted bail, suggesting that the relaxation of the bail requirement did not result in unacceptable default rates. Following this experiment, the New York Probation Department extended this program to criminal courts in all five boroughs of the city.

The classic research design consists of four essential features: comparison, manipulation, control, and generalizability.

Comparison

The process of comparison underlies the concept of covariation between a policy and its target variables. Suppose a relationship exists between policy A and the rates of unemployment. One would then expect to find a joint occurrence of both the policy and certain rates of unemployment; that is, political systems will have lower unemployment rates after implementing the policy than before. Similarly, political systems that implement the policy will have lower unemployment rates than political systems that do not. Thus, to assess the joint occurrence of a policy and changes in the target variables, a comparison is made of a group that was introduced to the policy with one that was not, or of the group's scores on the target variables before and after implementation of the policy. In the former case, an experimental group is compared with a comparison group; in the latter, an experimental group is compared with itself.

Manipulation

The notion of policy effectiveness implies that a policy has changed, and usually improved, certain conditions. A program such as Head Start is supposed to improve the cognitive skills of children participating in it. In other words, if a policy is actually effective, individuals introduced to the policy should change over the time of participation. The assumption that in the real world there are certain agents that produce change has its counterpart in the laboratory experiment in which the researcher actually acts as such an agent. The idea is that "if X is a cause of Y, and if it were possible to hold constant all other causes of Y, an experimental manipulation of the independent variable X (i.e., an externally produced change in X) should be accompanied by an observed change in Y."[2] The change in Y (the target variable) may not occur before the change in X (the policy) if one is to infer that Y is caused by X.

Control: Internal Validity

The third essential feature of the classic experimental design is that other factors be ruled out as rival explanations of the observed relationship between a policy and its target variables, as such factors might invalidate inferences concerning causality. Donald T. Campbell and Julian C. Stanley have formulated this as the problem of internal validity,[3] referring to the degree to which a research design allows the researcher to rule out alternative explanations for the way a particular policy is causally related to its target variables. The factors that may jeopardize internal validity can be classified as those which are extrinsic to the research operation and those which are intrinsic and impinge upon the results during the study period.

Sources of Internal Invalidity   Extrinsic factors are possible biases resulting from differential recruitment of individuals to the experimental and comparison groups. As an illustration, consider F. Stuart Chapin's study on the social effects of public housing.[4] This investigation was an early attempt to examine the changes occurring in the social lives of slum families as a result of their rehousing in public housing projects. Chapin compared an experimental group of families who had been rehoused with a comparison group of families who were still living under slum conditions. The main finding of the study showed a marked improvement in the social lives of those in the experimental group, leading to the inference that public housing projects change the life styles of their inhabitants. However, a rival explanation of the observed change in the rehoused families is that the people in new housing projects were initially different from the families serving as a comparison group. Perhaps the groups differed in type of employment, level of education, family size, or attitudes. These factors could also account for the observed differences between the two groups. Selection factors such as these must be controlled before the investigator can rule them out as rival interpretations.

Selection effects are especially salient and problematic if the individuals themselves decide whether to participate in a program. In such cases, the investigator cannot tell whether the policy itself caused the observed differences between the experimental and comparison groups or whether other variables related to the selection procedures were responsible for the observed effects. Peter H. Rossi, among others, points out that many social programs, once put into effect, are available on a self-selection basis to a larger target population.[5] Assessment of the effectiveness of such programs is more problematic because of such selection effects.

Intrinsic factors, on the other hand, are changes that occur during the investigation period, changes in the measuring instruments, or the reactive effects of the study itself. Following are the major intrinsic factors that might invalidate causal inferences.[6]

Historical factors are events that occur during the time of the investigation that might affect the cases or the individuals being studied and provide rival explanations for the change in the target variables. The longer the time lapse between the preprogram and the postprogram measurements, the higher the probability that historical events will become potential rival hypotheses. For example, in a study attempting to assess the effect of an energy conservation campaign on consumer behavior, the hypothesis might be that propaganda to which consumers are exposed during the campaign is likely to influence their behavior. The behavior of consumers is compared before and after exposure to propaganda. Yet differences in preprogram and postprogram behavior could result from events that occurred during this period, for instance, increased energy costs, government regulations, or irregular weather conditions.

A second group of factors that may become plausible rival hypotheses is designated *maturation* and includes processes that produce change merely as a function of the passage of time. Such changes could possibly influence the target variable and confound the research findings. Suppose an investigator wants to evaluate the effect of a specific teaching program on student achievement and records students' achievement before and after the program has been implemented. Between the preprogram and postprogram measurements, however, students have grown older; this change, unrelated to the teaching program, could possibly explain the difference between the two measurements. Processes such as growth and fatigue can produce changes in the target variable independently of the program.

The processes of *testing* and *measuring* may themselves change the phenomena being studied. This reactivity of measurement is a major problem in assessing the effectiveness of policies and programs. The effect of being tested prior to the introduction of a program might sensitize individuals and improve their scoring on the postprogram measurement. A difference between postprogram and preprogram scores could thus be attributed not necessarily to the program but rather to the experience gained by individuals in the preprogram phase. For example, an ineffective program to improve cognitive skills could report improvement if identical tests were used in the preprogram and postprogram phases since individuals might remember items or questions and discuss them before taking the postprogram test. One might question whether a program would have the same effect if the preprogram test had not sensitized individuals to the program objectives.

Instrument decay refers to changes in the measuring procedures or instruments between the preprogram and postprogram measurements. To associate the difference between postprogram and preprogram scores with the program, the researcher must assume that repeated measurements with the same instrument under constant conditions will yield the same results. If such an assumption cannot be made, observed differences could be attributed to the change in the measurement instrument and not necessarily to the policy (see chapter four). For example, if a program to improve cognitive skills were evaluated by comparing preprogram and postprogram ratings by psychologists, any changes in the psychologists' standards of judgment that occurred between testing periods would bias the findings.

Regression artifacts are pseudoshifts that occur when individuals have been selected on the basis of their extreme scores on the preprogram measures. Regression effects "guarantee that individuals who scored below average on a pretest will appear to have improved upon retesting."[7] Conversely, if the measuring instrument is not perfectly reliable, individuals who scored above the average on the preprogram test would appear to have done less well upon retesting.[8]

Experimental mortality is the differential loss of individuals from the experimental and comparison groups. Such differential loss may create observed differences in the postprogram scores that cannot be attributed to the policy. For example, in a study of the effect of the media on prejudice, if most dropouts were prejudiced individuals, the impression rendered could be that exposure to media reduced prejudice, whereas in fact it was the effect of experimental mortality that produced the observed shift in opinion.

Selection-maturation interaction refers to the selection of individuals who will change between the preprogram and postprogram measurements regardless of whether they participate in a program.

Randomization   Research designs such as the classic experimental design and those to be discussed in the next section provide control against extrinsic and intrinsic sources of internal invalidity. Ideally, the comparison and experimental groups are under identical conditions during the study, except for their differential exposure to the program (individuals in the comparison group do not participate in the program). Consequently, features of the research situation or external events that occur during the investigation are likely to influence the two groups equally and will not be confounded with the effects of the policy. For example, history cannot remain a rival hypothesis if the experimental and comparison groups are both exposed to the same events occurring during the study. Similarly, maturation is neutralized if the two groups undergo the same changes. Although the inclusion of a comparison group does not necessarily avoid the problem of experimental mortality, since the loss of cases might be differential and bias the results, an acceptable procedure is to include in the final sample only cases for which complete information is available.[9] Thus, the perfect experimental research design is one in which all the factors likely to affect the outcome of the program are controlled.

In practice, approximations to the perfect experiment are attempted through the method of randomization.[10] *Randomization* refers to the assignment of individuals (or other units of analysis, for example, groups, cities, states) of a target population to experimental and comparison groups in such a way that for any given assignment to a group, every member of the target population has an equal, nonzero probability of being selected for that assignment.

In other words, the underlying rationale of randomization is that since in random procedures every member of a target population has an equal, nonzero chance of being chosen, members with certain distinct attributes (lower or upper social class, white or black, urban or rural areas, and so on) will, if selected, be counterbalanced in the long run by the selection of other members of the target population with the "opposite" quality or quantity of the attribute.

Effective randomization makes a study unbiased, since it can have no a priori tendency to favor one group of experimental individuals over another. In large policy experiments, randomization tends to equate groups with respect to all possible antecedent factors. In addition, randomization permits a valid estimate of variability due to error, which is needed to specify the stability of inference.[11]

Generalizability: External Validity

Internal validity is indeed a crucial aspect of policy evaluation research. An additional significant question concerns the extent to which the research findings can be generalized to larger populations and applied to different settings. This problem is termed the external validity of research designs. Two issues of external validity involve the representativeness of the sample and the reactive arrangements in the research procedure.

Representativeness of the Sample   The random assignment of individuals to experimental and comparison groups does assure equivalence between the groups and thus contributes to the internal validity of the study. However, it does not necessarily assure representativeness of the population of interest. Results that prove to be internally valid might be specific to the sample selected for the particular study. This possibility becomes likely when recruitment of individuals to the experiment is difficult. Consider an experiment on college students that is carefully planned yet is based on volunteers. This sample cannot be assumed to be representative of the student body, let alone of the general population. To permit generalizations beyond the limited scope of the specific study, care should be taken to select the sample using a sampling frame that assures representation. Probability methods such as random sampling make generalizations to larger and clearly defined populations possible.[12]

Reactive Arrangements   The results of a study are to be generalized not only to a larger population but also to a real-life setting. This cannot always be accomplished, especially when a study is carried out in a highly artificial and contrived environment. In addition to the possible artificiality of the experimental setting, various features in the setting might be reactive and affect the external validity of the study. For example, preprogram measurement may influence the responsiveness of individuals to the experimental stimulus (the program); the observed effect would thus be specific to a population that has been measured at the preprogram phase.

Research designs can be classified by the extent to which they meet the criteria discussed thus far. Some designs allow for manipulation but fail to employ methods of control or an adequate sampling plan; others may include comparison groups but have no control over the manipulation of a policy. Accordingly, three major types of designs can be distinguished: experimental, quasi-experimental, and pre-experimental. In experimental designs, individuals or other units of analysis are randomly assigned to the experimental and comparison groups and the policy is introduced only to the experimental group. Such designs allow for comparison, control, manipulation, and, in most cases, generalizability. Quasi-experimental designs usually include combinations of some of these elements but not all of them. Typically these designs lack possibilities for manipulation and randomization. Pre-experimental designs include even fewer safeguards than quasi-experimental designs, and in this sense they provide the least assurance as to whether a policy is effective. Experimental designs are discussed in the next sections; pre-experimental and quasi-experimental designs will be presented in chapter three.

CONTROLLED EXPERIMENTATION

The classic experimental design presented at the beginning of this chapter is one of the strongest models of proof. It allows for preprogram and postprogram measurements and comparison group–experimental group comparisons; it permits the manipulation of a policy or a program; and, by including randomized groups, it controls for most sources of internal invalidity. However, the classic experimental design is relatively weak on external validity. Two variations of this design are stronger in this respect: the Solomon Four-Group design and the Postprogram-Only Comparison Group design.

The Solomon Four-Group Design

Preprogram measurement in an experimental setting has both advantages and disadvantages. Although it provides an assessment of the time sequence as well as a basis of comparison, it can have severe reactive effects. By sensitizing the sampled population, a preprogram test might in and of itself affect experimental results. For example, measuring public attitudes toward a government policy prior to its implementation may sensitize individuals to respond differently than nonpretested persons would. Further, preprogram measurements might be impractical in some circumstances.

The Solomon Four-Group design, presented in Table 2.2, where R represents randomized assignments, contains the same features as the classic design, plus an additional set of comparison and experimental groups that are not measured prior to introduction of the program.[13] Therefore, the reactive effect of measurement can be directly assessed by comparing the two experimental groups (O_2 and O_5) and the two comparison groups (O_4 and O_6). The comparisons will indicate whether X (the policy) had an independent effect on the groups that were not sensitized by preprogram measurement procedures. If it can be shown that the policy had an effect even in the absence of preprogram measure-

Table 2.2   **The Solomon Four-Group Design**

	Before		After
R	O_1	X	O_2
R	O_3		O_4
R		X	O_5
R			O_6

ments, the results can be generalized to target populations that were not measured prior to the introduction of X. Moreover, as Campbell and Stanley suggest, "not only is generalizability increased, but in addition, the effect of X is replicated in four different fashions: $O_2 > O_1$, $O_2 > O_4$, $O_5 > O_6$ and $O_5 > O_3$. The actual instabilities of experimentation are such that if these comparisons are in agreement, the strength of the inference is greatly increased."[14]

More recently, Robert E. Lana has demonstrated through a series of experiments that across a wide variety of attitudes and opinions, either (1) there was no difference in experimental effects between pretested and posttested-only groups, or (2) where differences were found, smaller changes occurred for the pretested than for the posttested-only groups. If anything, preprogram measurements tended to result in underestimates rather than in overestimates of effects.[15] In the context of policy evaluation research, these findings lead to the general conclusion that while preprogram sensitization may logically threaten the internal and external validity of policy experiments, the actual effects are rather small.[16]

The Postprogram-Only Comparison Group Design

Although the Solomon Four-Group design is a strong experimental design, such an elaborate plan is often impractical, too costly, or the pretests might be reactive. The Postprogram-Only Comparison Group design is a variation of both the classic design and the Solomon design; it omits the pretested groups altogether. The design is diagramed in Table 2.3. It is identical to that of the last two groups of the Solomon Four-Group design, which are not pretested. Individuals are randomly assigned to either the experimental or the comparison group and are measured during or after implementation of the policy.

Table 2.3
**The Postprogram-Only
Comparison Group Design**

		After
R	X	O_1
R		O_2

Suppose, for example, that a researcher examining the effects of a racist film on racial prejudice selects a sample of people who are randomly assigned to either of the two groups. One group is shown the film, and later both groups are interviewed and their responses compared. The occurrence of prejudice in the experimental group is compared with its occurrence in the comparison group. A significant difference will indicate that the film had an effect on prejudice. The time order can be inferred from the randomization process used to assign the individuals to the different groups. This procedure removes any initial differences between the groups, and it can therefore be inferred that the observed difference was caused by the program (film).

The Postprogram-Only Comparison Group design controls for all intrinsic sources of invalidity. With the omission of the pretest, testing and instrument decay become irrelevant sources of invalidity. It can also be assumed that the remaining intrinsic factors are controlled, since both groups are exposed to the same external events and undergo the same maturational processes. In addition, the extrinsic factor of selection is controlled by the random assignment of individuals, which removes an initial bias in either group.

Factorial Designs

The term *factorial design* refers to controlled experiments that involve more than one program variable and in which the several program variables (or factors) are orthogonal. Orthogonal means that each of the levels of each factor is manipulated or administered in combination with each of the levels of the others. Factorial designs, then, elaborate the number of experimental and comparison groups because, as Ronald A. Fisher has suggested:

> We are usually ignorant which, out of the innumerable possible factors, may prove ultimately to be the most important, though we may have strong presuppositions that some few of them are particularly worthy of study. We have equally no knowledge that any one factor will exert its effects independently of all others, or that its effects are particularly simply related to variations in these other factors.[17]

Factorial designs set up each possible combination of the program variables. For example, a factorial experiment involving three program variables is the same as three separate experiments, each of which investigates a different one of these variables. However, in three separate experiments three different samples would be employed, whereas a factorial experiment requires a single sample only slightly larger than that of any one of the separate experiments.

The chief advantage of factorial experiments is that they may considerably broaden the range of generalizability. Instead of "controlling for everything," as in single-variable experiments, additional relevant variables are introduced, each at two or more different levels. Consequently, the researcher is not restricted by some constant level of each of these relevant variables when generalizing on the effect of a policy. Rather, the investigator is in a position to infer that the effect of a policy occurs similarly across several levels of the variables or, alternatively, that the effect is different at different levels of one or another of these variables.

In factorial experiments the effect of one of the program variables at a single level of another of the variables is referred to as the simple effect. The overall effect of a program variable averaged across all the levels of the remaining program variables is referred to as its main effect. Interaction describes the manner in which the simple effects of a variable may differ from level to level of other variables. For example, if the simple effects of a variable, A, differ significantly from level to level of another variable, B, this is expressed by showing that the interaction between A and B was significant.

To exemplify the logic of factorial designs, consider a policy experiment involving two orthogonal factors, A and B, each with two levels—a_1 and a_2 and b_1 and b_2—(this is termed a 2^2 design). Figure 2.1 illustrates the design of this experiment and the resulting four combinations. Suppose two communities have been assigned at random to each of these four cells. This implies that each community will get a combination of two experimental manipulations, but each pair of communities will get a different combination. Now it is possible to conceive the factors as being independent—two separate experiments actually being administered with the same sample. In one experiment program A is being manipulated, and in the other program B.

The main effect of B is contained in the difference between

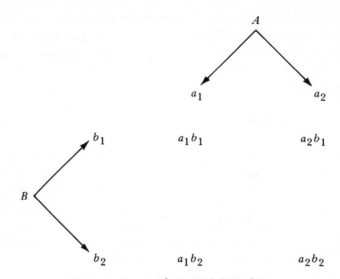

Figure 2.1   **A 2^2 Factorial Design**

the mean ($\bar{X}$) of cells a_1b_1 and a_2b_1 combined versus the mean of cells a_1b_2 and a_2b_2 combined. Similarly, the main effect of A is contained in the difference between the mean of cells a_1b_1 and a_1b_2 combined versus the mean of cells a_2b_1 and a_2b_2 combined. The simple effect of B with a_1 involves the difference between the a_1b_1 and the a_1b_2 cell means, whereas the simple effect of B with a_2 involves the difference between the a_2b_1 and the a_2b_2 cell means. The difference between these two differences defines the $B \times A$ interaction:

$$(\bar{X}_{a_1b_1} - \bar{X}_{a_1b_2}) - (\bar{X}_{a_2b_1} - \bar{X}_{a_2b_2}) \tag{2.1}$$

Similarly, the interaction in terms of the difference between the two simple effects of A at the two levels of B results in:

$$(\bar{X}_{a_1b_1} - \bar{X}_{a_2b_1}) - (\bar{X}_{a_1b_2} - \bar{X}_{a_2b_2}) \tag{2.2}$$

Each of these two descriptions of the $A \times B$ interaction simplifies to:

$$(\bar{X}_{a_1b_1} + \bar{X}_{a_2b_2}) - (\bar{X}_{a_2b_1} + \bar{X}_{a_1b_2}) \tag{2.3}$$

indicating that the interaction consists of a contrast of the two pair-combinations which lie opposite each other on the diagonals of the experimental scheme.[18]

TYPES OF EXPERIMENTS

Policy experimentation can be carried out either in the laboratory or in the field. The two settings share a common concern. In both, the investigator attempts to establish causal relationships by maximizing control over extrinsic and intrinsic factors while employing one of the various experimental designs and systematically recording observations. The major considerations involved with laboratory experimentation in the context of policy evaluation research will be discussed first.

Laboratory Experiments

Laboratory experimentation involves the introduction of conditions in a controlled environment (the laboratory) that simulates certain features of a natural environment. It allows the construction of a situation with closely supervised manipulation of one or more variables at a time to observe the effects produced.

One critical question with regard to laboratory experiments concerns their meaningfulness to policy evaluation research since they do not represent real-life situations. Indeed, in everyday life it is almost inconceivable that situations will be found that approximate the laboratory. But some years ago, Elliot Aronson and J. Merrill Carlsmith suggested two senses in which any given laboratory experiment can be said to be realistic.[19] In one sense, an experiment is realistic if the situation is realistic to the individual participating in it, if it involves that individual and has an impact on him or her. This kind of realism is commonly termed *experimental realism*. The second sense refers to the extent to which events that occur in a laboratory setting are likely to occur in the real world. This type of realism is referred to as *mundane realism*. In principle, an experiment that is high on mundane realism and low on experimental realism does not necessarily yield more meaningful results than one that is high on experimental realism and low on mundane realism. Experimental realism enables the researcher to increase the internal validity of the experiment by producing within the experimental situation a significant effect that would usually be extremely difficult to produce in natural environments.

Although laboratory experiments operationalize the idea of controlled experimentation in the sense that they are studies in which "(1) an investigator interferes with a process, so that (2) random subsets of the units processed are differently treated, and (3) measurements are collected in such a way that variability among units which were treated the same way can be estimated,"[20] they have certain limitations. These can be classified into three types: bias due to the demand characteristics of the experimental situation itself; bias due to the unintentional influence of the experimenters; and measurement artifacts.

Demand Characteristics   Bias due to demand characteristics comes about when individuals know that they are in an experimental situation and are aware that they are being observed and that certain responses are expected from them.[21] Consequently, individuals may not respond to the experimental manipulation as such, but to their interpretation of what responses these manipulations are supposed to elicit from them. Even if the individual is "told that there are no right or wrong responses, he knows that there are answers that will enhance or diminish his value as a person in the experimenter's eyes."[22] The individual may discover the research hypothesis and respond in a manner consistent with it in an attempt to cooperate with the experimenter. One common way to reduce this source of bias is through deception. Individuals are not told the true objective of the experiment but some other credible hypothesis. Thus, if a person modifies behavior so as to support or refute an incorrect hypothesis, the results relating to the true hypothesis might not be affected in a systematic way.[23]

Experimenter Bias   Behavior of the experimenter that is not intended to be part of the experimental manipulation but that nevertheless influences individuals who participate in an experiment is termed experimenter bias. When experimenters know what effects they desire from individuals, they may inadvertently communicate their expectations in various ways, for example by showing tension or relief on occasion, or by nodding the head. Robert Rosenthal and his colleagues found that when eight of twelve experimenters testing subjects on the same assignment received biased data from their first two subjects (who were accomplices of Rosenthal and his coinvestigators), these early returns influenced the data they collected from subsequent true subjects. The four experimenters who received hypothesis-confirming data from their first two subjects obtained the strongest confirming data from naïve subjects who followed the planted subjects. The four experimenters who received disconfirming data from their first two subjects obtained the most disconfirming data from the naïve subjects who served after the plants. The comparison group of experimenters, who ran only naïve subjects, obtained values between those obtained by the other two groups of experimenters. Accordingly, it was concluded that early returns bias subsequently obtained data.[24]

Attempts to minimize the occurrence of unintentional experimenter bias are directed toward eliminating communication of expectations by using automated procedures such as tape recorders or television cameras that tend to minimize interactions between experimenter and subject. The underlying rationale of such procedures is that bias effects may be reduced if individuals do not interact with the experimenters. Bias effects have also been handled through the use of experimenters with differing expectations regarding the outcome of the investigation. For example, in one study experimenters with different expectations about the effects of the manipulated variables were included as one of the variables in the experimental design. In this case, the researchers assessed whether their own differing expectations produced different outcomes.[25]

Measurement Artifacts   Measurement is a crucial part of the research process. In laboratory experiments and policy experiments in general, where the effects of a program are often subtle, sensitive and precise measurement is needed to detect such effects. Moreover, measurement procedures are not independent of research design problems, as measurement procedures may create additional interpretations of the obtained data by giving persons who participate in an experiment additional ideas about what is going on, by giving an individual a chance to present himself or herself in a favorable light, and so on. For example, measuring an attitude may moderate extreme attitudes by showing individuals that less extreme attitudes are prevalent. Furthermore, standardized measurement instruments (questionnaires, interviews, observations) may be perceived differently by different populations. Although standardized instruments add to the generalizability of results if they can be confirmed with different populations, the generalizability of the relation gains even more substantial increment when replications employ nonstandardized measurement instruments.[26]

Measuring instruments may be reactive in the sense that they may change the phenomenon being measured. For instance, the use of cameras in the presence of experimenters may cause the individuals being studied to behave atypically. Relatedly, exposure to the measuring instrument in a pretest may sensitize individuals and affect their posttest scores. Finally, the time of measurement may produce misleading results. That is, a researcher may measure for the effects of program variables before they have time to materialize or after they have already waned, thus concealing the actual effect. Carl I. Hovland and his co-workers, for example, found that discredited speakers have no immediate persuasive effect on their listeners, but may have a significant effect a month later, unless the listeners are reminded of the source.[27]

Field Experiments

The major difference between laboratory experimentation and experiments in the field is, as the terms imply, the setting. A field experiment is carried out in a natural environment with the researcher manipulating a program under as carefully controlled conditions as the situation permits. In terms of research designs, the contrast between the laboratory experiment and the field study is not sharp; differences are matters of degree. However, the difficulties involved in controlling extrinsic and intrinsic factors are considerably greater in field experiments.

The New Jersey Negative Income Tax Experiment   One important application of field experimentation has been the New Jersey Negative Income Tax Experiment, which evolved from the negative income tax concept, one of a number of guaranteed-income proposals suggested as replacements for other, unsatisfactory, welfare programs.[28] The virtues of a negative income tax were advocated as simplicity of administration; equity (it is paid to all whose incomes fall below a prescribed level); dignity (there are no indiscriminate investigations); and the creation of conditions conducive to individual initiative (the negative tax grant is not taken away from a recipient dollar for dollar as his earned income increases).

The way the scheme works is rather simple. An individual or family whose earned income is zero is granted a standard amount of money (the "guarantee"). No matter what the family does with the money, the family income will never fall below the guaranteed amount. If the family earns additional income of its own, the initial guaranteed income is reduced at some established rate. As the family increases its earnings, the guaranteed amount continues to be reduced until the family reaches a point at which the guarantee has been completely used up (the "breakeven point"). Beyond this point, the family receives no more supplementary funds unless and until its income falls below the breakeven point again, in which event the supplement would again be paid according to the same formula.

The major issues with the negative income tax idea concern work incentive and cost, the latter being dependent on the former. If all families in the United States below the breakeven income tax level were eligible to participate in such a program, the target population would include many families with a partially or fully employed earner. The question then would be by what amount this earner's work effort would be reduced in response to the receipt of supplementary income. If this group of "working poor" were all included in a national income-maintenance program, the problem of work incentive would have become cardinal.

Given that there are many families with incomes between, say, $3,500 and $7,000, it was believed that a slight reduction in their work effort would have a strong impact on the cost of a national program. Consequently, a decision was made to evaluate the program using a number of select communities rather than the entire target population. For the experiment, 1,359 low-income, male-headed families in five metropolitan areas—Trenton, Paterson, Passaic, and Jersey City, New Jersey, and Scranton, Pennsylvania—were selected and randomly assigned to one of eight different negative tax plans or to a comparison group. The total number of families in the experimental groups was 725 and in the comparison group 634.

The sample families were interviewed once every three months throughout the three-year experiment. Each family in the experimental groups which filed an income report correctly received a check in the mail every two weeks. The amount of the check was computed using the family's negative tax plan and its income for the appropriate period. Each family also received $10 every two weeks to compensate them for the time and trouble expended in filling out reports. Experimental families who filed correctly continued to receive payments even if they moved to other parts of the country, and all families continued to be interviewed even if they moved elsewhere in the country. Families which broke up continued to receive payments separately as new filing units. "Each year the experiment administers 5000, 350-question interviews, writes over $800,000 in checks to experimental families, processes 10,000 family Income Report Forms and adds over 30 million words of data to the computer records."[29] The design of the experiment is shown in Table 2.4.

Table 2.4   **Research Design of the New Jersey Negative Income Tax Experiment***

Groups	Guarantee (% of Poverty Line)	Tax Rate (%)
Experimental groups		
A	50	30
B	50	50
C	75	30
D	75	50
E	75	70
F	100	50
G	100	70
H	125	50
Comparison group	0	0

* A negative income tax plan was defined by a guarantee level (the level of payment the family receives if its other income is zero) and a tax or benefit reduction rate (the rate at which the payment is reduced for each dollar of income). Eight such negative income tax plans were chosen for the experiment (combinations of three tax rates and four guarantee levels).

Two distinct but interrelated issues are involved with field experimentation in general and with the New Jersey experiment in particular. One is concerned with control over extrinsic and intrinsic factors, or with validity issues; the other concerns problems of implementing the intended experiment in the field.

Validity Issues   The chief advantage of field experiments is that they are appropriate for investigating complex phenomena, processes, and changes, in natural settings. However, their main weakness is that of control; control of intrinsic and especially of extrinsic factors is rarely as complete as in laboratory experiments. Although researchers can in principle manipulate a policy and randomize groups, they are nevertheless faced with the possibility that the program variables are contaminated by uncontrolled environmental factors.

To meet such problems, several procedures have been suggested. First, whenever possible, the experiment should be replicated. For example, the Institute for Research on Poverty has executed a negative income tax experiment for rural areas. Replication serves two interrelated objectives: (1) it establishes the validity of previous findings, and (2) it helps in determining the generalizability of the findings under different conditions. Each time the same findings are obtained under different conditions, not only is the generalizability of the findings extended, but confidence in the validity of these findings is increased as well. Second, if replication is not intended or is not feasible, pilot field experiments should be conducted to ensure that the experimental manipulations produce observable variations. If the experimental manipulations are not sufficiently strong to produce differences, the field conditions must be simplified. In addition, it has been recommended that field experiments be applied to units of relatively small size and that the experimental manipulation be confined to relatively short time periods; longer periods increase the chances of unanticipated events.

Implementation Problems   One of the major difficulties with field experiments concerns their implementation, since they take place in a social-political context. Political considerations may pose difficulties at the implementation stage and bias the findings in various ways. For example, the New Jersey Negative Income Tax Experiment required substantial negotiations with the communities and considerable effort to preserve the integrity of the research design. In one community an entire public housing project refused to cooperate with the researchers until the latter found the "community leader" and got his approval. Such unofficial representatives of the various segments of the community are critical contacts during an entire experiment. In urban settings where competing power groups operate, this problem is, as David N. Kershaw observes, considerably more complicated:

> It is not enough, for example, to locate a Puerto Rican leader and consider the "Puerto Rican community" fully informed. It is often the case that intense rivalries exist within the community . . . , and between the community leaders and the previous peers who are now in local government positions. The important lesson here is that while the organization operating the experiment should attempt to contact various groups and individuals within the local area, it should also be extremely careful not to be identified with them.[30]

The relationship between the investigators and other organizations and agencies poses different problems. With respect to the relationship between the organization that conducts the research and the various levels of government, the lesson of the New Jersey experiment has been that "unless the number of actors is kept to a minimum, substantial, and perhaps insurmountable, operational problems will arise . . . [the complexity of such experiments] means that the entire [research] organization must be kept extremely flexible."[31]

The other general lesson of the New Jersey experiment is that an organization conducting a field experiment should have no connection with local agencies or organizations at the experimental site. Kershaw notes that "on numerous occasions in New Jersey, the fact that the experiment was funded by OEO in *Washington* (as distinct from the local Community Action Agency, for example) got us out of very difficult situations."[32] Local groups attempt to influence the course of an experiment in various ways. In the New Jersey experiment such groups wanted to have a say in the selection of the sample. However, the fact that the experiment was not funded by local organizations and the continuing emphasis on its scientific nature helped minimize such intrusions.

Henry W. Riecken and Robert F. Boruch have suggested a number of critical operational problems that have to be dealt with in the implementation stage. These are general tasks, not specific to certain research topics or to a particular setting.[33] First, the management of a field experiment must assume responsibility for the negotiations required to implement the experimental design, aiming:

> to develop a set of operational objectives and a set of measures related to those objectives on which parties to the experiment agree; to reconcile the value differences as much as possible and minimize the potential conflicts between action team and researchers; and to develop a harmoniously functioning staff that will be governed by high standards of quality in the execution of the experiment.[34]

Second, the management has to develop the details of the research design and good working relationships with the community in which the experiment takes place. Third, the management has to maintain the integrity of the design while allowing a certain amount of flexibility in its detail to meet unanticipated occurrences. Last, the management must establish and constantly supervise procedures to ensure the quality of the data collected. Indeed, failure to handle such problems adequately would be reflected in the quality of the research findings and in their policy implications.

Notwithstanding the implementation problems and the validity threats that might be involved in policy experimentation, experimental research designs provide the most convincing evidence concerning the causal effects of policies: "The capacity to produce a particular outcome deliberately in a randomly assigned group of persons is the surest testimony of the effectiveness of the treatment."[35] Furthermore, John P. Gilbert, Richard J. Light, and Frederick Mosteller, after reviewing the research designs and findings of studies of almost forty social, medical, and sociomedical programs, observed that few of the studies reported marked positive effects. Even programs "that turned out to be especially valuable often had relatively small effects—gains of a few percent, for example, or larger gains for a small subgroup of the population treated. Because even small gains accumulated over time can sum to a considerable total, they may have valuable consequences for society."[36] Not only are such small effects difficult to detect and measure, they also call for well-designed and well-executed evaluations: "Randomization, together with careful control and implementation, gives an evaluation a strength and persuasiveness that cannot ordinarily be obtained by other means."[37]

NOTES

1. The following account leans on Bernard Botein, "The Manhattan Bail Project: Its Impact in Criminology and the Criminal Law Process," *Texas Law Review*, 43 (February 1965), 319–331; and Henry W. Riecken and Robert F. Boruch, eds., *Social Experimentation: A Method for Planning and Evaluating Social Intervention* (New York: Academic Press, 1974), pp. 1–2.
2. Hubert M. Blalock, Jr., *Causal Inferences in Nonexperimental Research* (Chapel Hill: University of North Carolina Press, 1964), p. 22.
3. Donald T. Campbell and Julian C. Stanley, *Experimental and Quasi-Experimental Designs for Research* (Chicago: Rand McNally, 1966), p. 5.
4. F. Stuart Chapin, "An Experiment on the Social Effects of Good Housing," *American Sociological Review*, 5 (December 1940), 868–879.
5. Peter H. Rossi, "Testing for Success and Failure in Social Action," in Peter H. Rossi and Walter Williams, eds., *Evaluating Social Programs* (New York: Seminar Press, 1972), pp. 11–49.
6. The following discussion is based on Campbell and Stanley, *Experimental and Quasi-Experimental Designs for Research*; and Donald T. Campbell, "Reforms as Experiments," *American Psychologist*, 24 (April 1969), 409–429.
7. Tom R. Houston, Jr., "The Behavioral Sciences Impact-Effectiveness Model," in Rossi and Williams, eds., *Evaluating Social Programs*, p. 60.
8. A more detailed discussion of regression is presented in chapter five.
9. David Nachmias and Chava Nachmias, *Research Methods in the Social Sciences* (New York: St. Martin's, 1976), p. 34.
10. Matching is another procedure used. For its advantages, but especially its limitations, see Jim C. Nunnally, "The Study of Change in Evaluation Research: Principles Concerning Measurement, Experimental Design, and Analysis," in Elmer L. Struening and Marcia Guttentag, eds., *Handbook of Evaluation Research*, I (Beverly Hills, Calif.: Sage, 1975), pp. 130–131.
11. For an error interpretation of randomization, see William G. Cochran and Gertrude M. Cox, *Experimental Designs*, 2nd ed. (New York: Wiley, 1957), pp. 15–94.
12. For methods of securing representative samples, see Nachmias and Nachmias, *Research Methods in the Social Sciences*, chap. 12.

13. See Richard L. Solomon, "An Extension of Control Group Design," *Psychological Bulletin*, 46 (January 1949), 137–150.
14. Campbell and Stanley, *Experimental and Quasi-Experimental Designs for Research*, p. 25.
15. Robert E. Lana, "Pretest Sensitization," in Robert Rosenthal and Ralph L. Rosnow, eds., *Artifact in Behavioral Research* (New York: Academic Press, 1969), pp. 119–141.
16. See Ilene N. Bernstein et al., "External Validity and Evaluation Research," in Ilene N. Bernstein, ed., *Validity Issues in Evaluative Research*, Sage Contemporary Social Science Issues, XXIII (Beverly Hills, Calif.: Sage, 1976), p. 116.
17. Ronald A. Fisher, *The Design of Experiments* (Edinburgh: Oliver and Boyd, 1937), p. 101.
18. For more elaborated factorial designs, see Cochran and Cox, *Experimental Designs*.
19. Elliot Aronson and J. Merrill Carlsmith, "Experimentation in Social Psychology," in Gardner Lindzey and Elliot Aronson, eds., *The Handbook of Social Psychology*, I (Reading, Mass.: Addison-Wesley, 1968), pp. 1–79.
20. Houston, "The Behavioral Sciences Impact-Effectiveness Model," p. 52.
21. See Martin T. Orne, "On the Social Psychology of the Psychological Experiment: With Particular Reference to Demand Characteristics and Their Implications," *American Psychologist*, 17 (November 1962), 776–783.
22. Aronson and Carlsmith, "Experimentation in Social Psychology," p. 61.
23. For the ethical problems involved with deception, see Kai T. Erikson, "A Comment on Disguised Observation in Sociology," *Social Problems*, 14 (Spring 1967), 366–373.
24. Robert Rosenthal et al., "The Effect of Early Data Returns on Data Subsequently Obtained by Outcome-Biased Experimenters," *Sociometry*, 26 (December 1963), 487–498.
25. J. Merrill Carlsmith, Barry E. Collins, and Robert L. Helmreich, "Studies in Forced Compliance: I. The Effect of Pressure for Compliance on Attitude Change Produced by Face-to-Face Role Playing and Anonymous Essay Writing," *Journal of Personality and Social Psychology*, 4 (January 1966), 1–13.
26. See Paul C. Rosenblatt and Norman Miller, "Problems and Anxieties in Research Design and Analysis," in Charles G. McClintock, ed., *Experimental Social Psychology* (New York: Holt, Rinehart & Winston, 1972), pp. 68–69.
27. Carl I. Hovland, Irving L. Janis, and Harold H. Kelley, *Communication and Persuasion* (New Haven, Conn.: Yale University Press, 1953).
28. The following discussion leans on David N. Kershaw, "Issues in Income Maintenance Experimentation," in Rossi and Williams, eds., *Evaluating Social Programs*, pp. 221–245; and Robert H. Haveman and Harold W. Watts, "Social Experimentation as Policy Research: A Review of Negative Income Tax Experiments," in Gene V. Glass, ed., *Evaluation Studies: Review Annual*, I (Beverly Hills, Calif.: Sage, 1976), pp. 425–441.
29. Kershaw, "Issues in Income Maintenance Experimentation," p. 224.

30. Ibid., p. 226.
31. Ibid., p. 227.
32. Ibid.
33. Riecken and Boruch, *Social Experimentation*, pp. 153–201.
34. Ibid., p. 115.
35. Ibid., p. 22.
36. John P. Gilbert, Richard J. Light, and Frederick Mosteller, "Assessing Social Innovations: An Empirical Base for Policy," in Carl A. Bennett and Arthur A. Lumsdaine, eds., *Evaluation and Experiment: Some Critical Issues in Assessing Social Programs* (New York: Academic Press, 1975), pp. 39–40.
37. Ibid., p. 44.

Chapter Three

Quasi-Experimental Evaluations

The controlled experiment allows the most unequivocal assessment of the extent to which a policy exerts a causal impact on the target variables. However, the world in which decision makers operate is not always amenable to the straightforward application of experimental designs: social, political, and ethical considerations may impede the application of controlled experimentation. Therefore, considerable attention has recently focused on designing methods for policy evaluation when true experimentation is either impossible or impractical. One major development in this respect is the quasi-experimental design, in which one or more extrinsic and/or intrinsic variables are not controlled for. Typically this occurs when randomization cannot be achieved or when a comparison group is not feasible. To compensate for this weakness, supplementary data and specialized techniques of data analysis are used to reduce ambiguities of inference concerning the impact of a policy. To appreciate the relative causal inferential strengths of quasi-experimental designs, we will first discuss the shortcomings of three commonly employed pre-experimental designs.

PRE-EXPERIMENTAL DESIGNS

A very wanting form of pre-experimental design is:

$$X \qquad O_1$$

In this design a policy or public program (X) is applied and measurements (O_1) are carried out subsequently. For example, in January 1965 President Lyndon B. Johnson informed the public that a preschool program named Head Start would be established as part of the Community Action Program. Initially, $17 million were to be committed for the summer of 1965 to enable 100,000 children to participate.[1] The publicity given Head Start generated a large volume of demands for funds from numerous localities. The Office of Economic Opportunity (OEO) met these demands by committing $103 million to provide places for 560,000 children during the summer of 1965. Later in the year, Head Start was made a permanent part of the antipoverty program. According to President Johnson, Head Start had been "battle-tested" and "proven worthy" and, as a result, was expanded to include a full-year program. In 1968, $330 million were allocated to provide places for 473,000 children in summer programs and another 218,000 in full-year programs, turning Head Start into the largest single component of the Community Action Program.

As late as mid-1967, no reliable evidence existed regarding the effectiveness of the program. Members of Congress, the Bureau of the Budget, and OEO officials were, however, pressing for evidence. Consequently, the evaluation division of the Office of Research, Plans, Programs and Evaluations (RPP&E) proposed a study design for Head Start in which children who had participated in the program and were currently in the first, second, and third grades of school would be observed through a series of cognitive and affective tests. Performance on these tests would serve as evidence of the effectiveness of the program. Head Start officials opposed the proposed study on methodological and political grounds.[2]

Methodologically, such a pre-experimental design cannot provide solid evidence for inferring causality. There are numerous rival hypotheses that could explain differential performance in cognitive and affective tests, and for that matter in any other measures. First, measurements taken only at the observation period would have no meaningful basis of comparison, and comparison is an essential component for making causal inferences. The inferential capacity of this design can be somewhat improved if additional information is available. Accepted societal norms and standards may serve as a comparison base; for instance, national norms for achievement in various cognitive tests might be available from cross-sectional surveys to be used as a comparison base.

The other significant shortcoming of the above pre-experimental design is that it fails to provide any evidence of whether a policy had any impact on the target variables. To make valid causal inferences concerning the impact of a policy on its target variables, it is necessary to add, at least, measurements that were taken prior to implementation of the policy. This leads to the second pre-experimental design, commonly referred to as a preprogram-postprogram design:

$$O_1 \quad X \quad O_2$$

The obvious advantage of a preprogram-postprogram design is that the program's target variable is compared with itself: a target variable is measured before implementation of the program (O_1); after implementation the same target variable is measured again (O_2). The difference scores are examined to assess the causal impact of the program (X). In the case of Head Start, the children's performance, say on cognitive tests, could have been measured before their participation in the program and compared with the scores obtained after participation.

The major drawback of the preprogram-postprogram design is that changes in the target variables might have been produced by other events, not necessarily because of the policy. The longer the time lapse between the preprogram and postprogram measurements, the greater the chance of other variables' affecting the target variable and thus the postprogram measures. This possible source of invalidity was previously referred to as "history." The other shortcoming of this design is connected with changes in the target variable resulting from maturation. For example, the mental age of a child increases with time and this change can affect measures of cognitive performance.

A third possible source of invalidity in a preprogram-postprogram design concerns regression artifacts. These, as discussed earlier, are "Pseudo-shifts occurring when persons or treatment units have been selected upon the basis of their extreme scores."[3] This condition would exist if the investigated individuals had been preselected either (1) on the pretest independent variable, or (2) on some variable that correlates highly with the pretest variable. The first could occur, for example, if children for the Head Start program were selected initially because of their low performance in a reading test and the same test were used for the postprogram measure. The net effect in such a case might be that by chance factors lower scores on the preprogram would tend to be higher and higher scores lower on the postprogram when, in fact, no real change had taken place. The second possibility might occur if the children were selected not on the basis of performance on a reading test but on the basis of low scores on, say, an IQ test. Given that the two tests are highly correlated, the target group would be well below average on a reading performance test as well as on the IQ test. In general, it is expected that a regression artifact will occur when cases or units are selected because they are above or below average with respect to the preprogram and postprogram measures.[4]

The third commonly used pre-experimental design relies on postprogram measurement only but does employ a comparison group.[5] However, the experimental and comparison groups are not formed randomly from a larger representative population; instead, the groups are intact before implementation of the policy. This design can be symbolized as follows, with a dashed line between the rows representing the two groups indicating intact groups rather than randomly sampled ones:

$$X \qquad O_e$$
$$------$$
$$O_c$$

An example might compare the reading performance of children who participated in Head Start with the performance of a group of children who did not. The latter group is usually chosen to be as similar as possible to the group that was introduced to the policy.

One serious problem with this design is that individuals in the two groups might have differed initially with respect to the target variable measured (reading performance); that is, the groups were not equivalent before introduction of the program. Furthermore, possible differences between the groups might have occurred be-

cause of a greater willingness of members of one group to participate in the program (the "selection" source of invalidity). Nevertheless, evidence concerning the impact of a policy cannot be ruled
out altogether in cases where additional evidence shows that the
two groups do not differ significantly on the average in characteristics relating to the target variable.

The internal validity of these pre-experimental designs is weak;
too many critical intrinsic and extrinsic variables are not controlled
for. Therefore, inferences drawn from pre-experimental designs
regarding the causal effects of policies are inconclusive. Multivariate statistical analyses, such as the ones discussed in chapters five
and six, improve the inferential power of pre-experimental designs.

QUASI-EXPERIMENTAL DESIGNS

Keeping the classic experimental design as a model of proof, a
number of quasi-experimental designs have been developed.
Whereas these designs are weaker on internal validity than are
experimental designs, they provide considerably more internal validity than do pre-experimental designs. Unlike experimental designs that rule out the effects of influences other than exposure to
a policy, quasi-experimental designs do not require randomization
and often depend on the possibility that influences other than the
policy's variables can be ruled out by additional evidence and/or
data-analysis techniques. The major types of quasi-experimental
designs are discussed in the following sections.

Contrasted Groups Designs

A common problem in policy evaluation research is that in many
cases the researcher cannot randomly assign individuals or other
units of analysis to experimental and comparison groups. At times,
intact comparison groups are used either at the preprogram phase
only or at the postprogram phase. Causal inferences concerning
the effectiveness of a policy are especially vulnerable when groups
are compared that are known to differ in some important attributes, such as comparing poor communities with relatively well-to-
do ones, groups from different ethnic backgrounds, and males
with females. If a postprogram-only design is used with such con-

trasted groups, differences on the postprogram measures are likely to be due to initial differences between the groups rather than to the impact of a policy. Nevertheless, when differences among such contrasted groups are to be assessed, several elaborations in the research design are possible which can be regarded as safeguards against the intrusion of influences other than the program.

The least elaborated design for contrasted groups is that in which individuals or other units of analysis are regarded as members of categoric groups;[6] members of each group are measured with respect to the target variables. For example, one can compare the reading performances of children residing in different communities. This design can be symbolized in the following way:

$$O_a$$

$$O_b$$

$$O_c$$

$$O_d$$

.

.

.

$$O_k$$

Differences in measurement scores obtained for the above k groups are amenable to straightforward comparative statistical analyses (for example, difference between means). However, because such contrasted groups differ from one another in many ways, difficulties arise when attempts are made to assess the causes for the observed differences. Relatedly, the groups might differ because of artifacts in the measurement procedures rather than because of any real differences among them. For instance, it has been repeatedly shown that measurements based solely on personal interviews are affected by interviewers' backgrounds: if white interviewers interview both black and white respondents, the presence of the white interviewer might cause the black respondents to give answers that are not representative of their typical views.[7]

One way to reduce the risk of being wrong when making causal inferences based on Contrasted Groups designs is to obtain supplementary evidence over time regarding the hypothesized differences. Thus, if the same finding is obtained in other settings and comparisons are made on a number of measures concerning the target variables, then such supplementary evidence can increase the inferential powers of a Contrasted Groups design.

Another procedure that has been employed in comparing the effects of programs on contrasted groups is the matching of individuals from the two groups on one or more variables. Suppose, for example, that an evaluation is conducted of a new method of teaching reading skills in which a comparison is made between the degree of progress shown by children from an extremely poor neighborhood and the progress of children from a wealthy neighborhood in the same city. Preprogram measures show significant differences between the two groups before the introduction of the teaching method. The researcher combines pairs of children from the two groups whose scores on reading skills are very similar. With such a procedure, two groups are obtained that have similar average scores on the preprogram measures. But such a procedure can be vulnerable. By matching individuals in this manner, the researcher would be selecting children from a lower socioeconomic background with comparatively high scores on reading performance and children with comparatively low scores from higher socioeconomic backgrounds. Regardless of exposure to the program and because of the regression artifact, the findings would indicate that the reading performance of children from the lower socioeconomic background had declined, whereas children from the higher socioeconomic background had improved their reading skills. The major drawback of such a matching procedure is that the problem of whether individuals or other units of analysis have been matched on all relevant and significant factors that can invalidate causal inferences cannot be effectively dealt with.

In some cases in which contrasted groups are compared, measures are available on a number of occasions before and after implementation of a policy. In such cases multiple measures can be obtained before and/or after implementation. Such supplementary data provide a measure of the amount of normal variation in the target variable from time to time, irrespective of a policy's impact. Suppose, for example, that researchers wish to evaluate the effectiveness of a new approach to teaching reading implemented through the fifth grade in school E. They can compare achievement-test scores in reading for children in the third through seventh grades in that school and in another school (C) in the same community that did not use the new approach. The study is conducted retroactively for students who are currently in the seventh grade and have remained in school from the third grade up to that time. Because schools administer achievement tests each year, the researchers can obtain comparable measures for each of the five years. Evidence for a program effect when there are multiple measures over time consists of a sharp interaction from before to after implementation of a policy for the units being compared, as illustrated in Figure 3.1.

Unlike the hypothetical results in Figure 3.1, the findings shown in Figure 3.2 indicate that a policy had no effect at all on the individuals in group E beyond what could be expected from the usual course of events, as evidenced in group C. The apparent

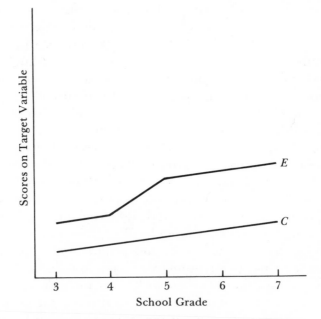

Figure 3.1 **Comparison of Two Contrasted Groups Indicating that the Program Had a Definite Effect**

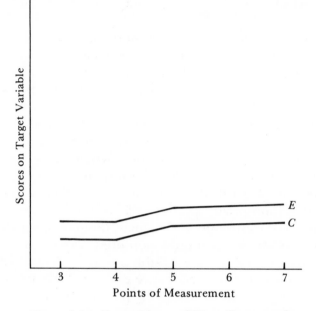

Figure 3.2   **Comparison of Two Contrasted Groups Indicating that a Policy Had No Effect**

change in group *E* is illusory because it is matched by a proportional change in group *C*. As Jim C. Nunnally suggests, unless striking findings are obtained, like those depicted in the figures, it is usually risky to make any firm inferences concerning the effectiveness of a policy from a Contrasted Groups design.[8]

Planned Variation Designs
Planned Variation designs involve exposure of individuals to systematically varying kinds of programs to assess the causal effects of the programs. The Head Start Planned Variation (HSPV) study exemplifies such designs. HSPV was a three-year investigation designed to compare the different effects that different kinds of Head Start centers were having on the development of the academic skills of children from relatively poor families. The study was developed on the assumption that by selecting "sponsors" for different types of programs, and by systematically varying the kinds of programs offered to children, it would be possible to

discover which kinds of programs most benefited which kinds of children.[9]

Sponsors selected to participate in the investigation had a substantial amount of variation in their goals and their teaching structures. During the 1971–1972 academic year, eleven sponsors were distributed over a total of twenty-eight sites. For purposes of comparison, eleven of the twenty-eight sites also had "nonsponsored" Head Start classrooms. In addition, three sites had comparison group children who were not enrolled in any program. Children for this comparison group were contacted by direct recruitment and from Head Start waiting lists. Each sponsor had two, three, or four sites. Within each site were variable numbers of classrooms run by the appropriate sponsor. Whereas some sites contained both sponsored classrooms and regular, nonsponsored Head Start classrooms, other sites had only sponsored classrooms.

One major shortcoming of this research design was that a number of important variables were not equally distributed across the sponsors. Herbert I. Weisberg points out that race, age of children, prior preschool experience, and socioeconomic background were all unequally distributed. For example, one sponsor had almost no black children at his site, while another sponsor had almost no white children. In spite of this serious source of invalidity, three general inferences were drawn: (1) overall, both the sponsors' programs and the regular Head Start programs tended to accelerate certain kinds of specific academic performance, such as number and letter recognition; (2) pooling the eleven sponsored sets of classrooms and comparing them with the regular, nonsponsored Head Start classrooms showed no large differences; and (3) when the sponsored sets of classrooms were compared among themselves, some differences in performance emerged on the several cognitive tests the children were given. In other words, certain types of curricula seemed to enhance different kinds of cognitive development.

Obviously these conclusions are suggestive at best, because of the unequal distributions of important variables across the sponsors. The confidence in findings obtained with Planned Variation designs can be increased to a certain extent if the distribution of important variables is equal among the various groups and if measures of the target variable are taken on a number of occasions before and after implementation of programs.

Time-Series Designs

In some cases when no comparison group is available for assessing the effectiveness of a policy, Time-Series designs—research designs in which preprogram and postprogram measures are available on a number of occasions before and after implementation of a policy—can be utilized. Usually the investigator attempts to obtain at least three sets of measures before and after implementation of the policy. A typical Time-Series design can be represented as follows:

$$O_1 \quad O_2 \quad O_3 \quad X \quad O_4 \quad O_5 \quad O_6$$

Employment of a Time-Series design makes it possible to separate reactive measurement effects from the effects of a policy. A Time-Series design also enables the researcher to see whether a policy has an effect over and above the reactive effects. The reactive effect shows itself at O_3; this can be compared with O_4. An increase at O_4 above the increase at O_3 can be attributed to the policy. A similar argument applies for the maturation source of invalidity.

But Donald T. Campbell and Julian C. Stanley maintain that history is the most serious problem with this design.[10] They argue that it is plausible that the policy did not produce a change in the target, but rather the change was caused by some other event or combination of events occurring during the implementation period. Indeed, if there are constantly recurring events other than the policy, causal inferences concerning its effectiveness are problematic at best. Nevertheless, in concrete research situations, influences other than the policy might show up between, say, O_2 and O_3, as well as between O_3 and O_4, making history less of a threat.

A classic study that illustrates the advantages as well as the problems involved with Time-Series designs is the evaluation of the Connecticut crackdown on speeding following a record number of traffic fatalities in 1955.[11] At the end of 1956 there had been 284 traffic deaths, compared with 324 the year before, a

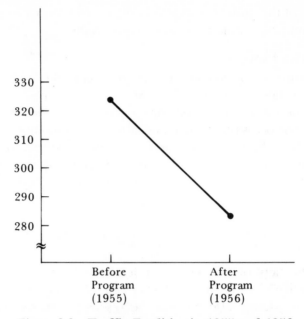

Figure 3.3   **Traffic Fatalities in 1955 and 1956**

reduction of 12.3 percent. The results are graphed in Figure 3.3, with the intention to magnify differences. Referring to these data, the authorities concluded that "the program is definitely worthwhile." Since this inference is based on a sort of preprogram-postprogram design, a number of plausible rival interpretations could also be advanced. For instance, 1956 might have been a particularly dry year, with fewer accidents due to rain or snow.

A more valid inference concerning the program's effectiveness can be made if the data are presented as part of an extended time series, as illustrated in Figure 3.4. This Time-Series design controls for maturation. The data permit the rejection of a rival interpretation suggesting that traffic death rates were already going down year after year, which could be a plausible interpretation if the measures were carried out only one year before and after implementation of the program.

Although the extended Time-Series design takes into account four observations before introduction of the program and three observations after its implementation, it nevertheless fails to control

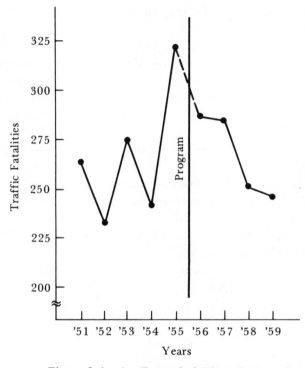

Figure 3.4 **An Extended Time Series of Traffic Fatalities**

Source: Donald T. Campbell, "Reforms as Experiments," *American Psychologist*, 24 (April 1969), 413. Reprinted by permission.

for the effects of other potential sources of invalidity; for example, history remains a plausible rival explanation. In such a case, one strategy for strengthening the credibility of the inference is to make use of supplementary data if these are available. For example, weather records can be examined to evaluate the rival interpretation that weather conditions were responsible for the decline in traffic deaths.

But time series are unstable even when no programs are being introduced. The degree of this normal instability is, according to Campbell, "the crucial issue, and one of the main advantages of the extended time-series is that it samples this instability."[12] In the Connecticut case the authorities had in fact implied that all the change from 1955 to 1956 was due to the crackdown policy.

However, as Figure 3.4 indicates, the relatively high preprogram instability makes the policy look ineffective: "The 1955–56 shift is less than the gains of both 1954–55 and 1952–53. It is the largest drop in the series, but it exceeds the drops of 1951–52, 1953–54, and 1957–58 by trivial amounts."[13] Accordingly, one can legitimately advance the argument that the 1955–1956 drop is merely a manifestation of series instabilities. Notwithstanding this plausible interpretation, it can be observed that after the crackdown there are no year-to-year gains, suggesting that the character of the time series has changed.[14]

Earlier, the notion of regression artifact as a source of invalidity was introduced. Regression artifact also presents a serious threat to the validity of Time-Series designs, especially when these are characterized by instabilities. As a rule it is maintained that with any highly variable time series, if one selects a point that is the "highest so far," the next point, on the average, will be lower, or nearer to the general trend. In the previous example the most dramatic shift in the whole series is the upward shift just prior to

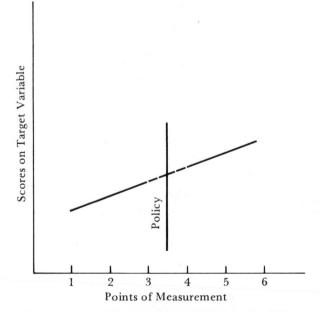

***Figure 3.5*   A Time Series Indicating No Effect of a Policy**

the crackdown. Thus it is plausible that this caused the implementation of the program, rather than, or in addition to, the program's causing the 1956 decline in traffic fatalities. Therefore, at least part of the 1956 drop is an artifact of the 1955 extremity.

Figure 3.5 illustrates a case from which it can be concluded that a policy had no effect on the target variable. The curve goes up from before the introduction of a policy to after its implementation. However, the curve was going up at the same rate before the introduction and continues up at the same rate after implementation. Interpretation of the hypothetical data in Figure 3.6 is more problematic. The curve goes up from the introduction of the policy to after its implementation. However, the great variations before introduction of the policy as well as those observed after its implementation provide no confidence concerning the causal effects of the policy.

Figures 3.5 and 3.6 illustrate but two different types of findings that could be obtained from a Time-Series study. They do, however, demonstrate again that Time-Series designs, as well as other quasi-experimental designs without any comparison group, provide only partial evidence concerning the causal effects of a policy.

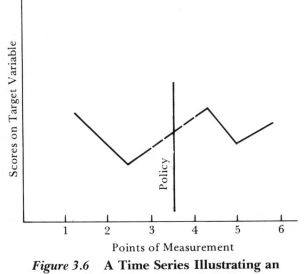

Figure 3.6   **A Time Series Illustrating an Illusory Effect of a Policy**

Control-Series Designs

It has already been pointed out that one of the major obstacles in constructing experimental designs for policy evaluation is the difficulty of applying random selection procedures in assigning individuals or other units of analysis to experimental and comparison groups. Procedures for matching might also be vulnerable when evidence concerning significant external factors is unavailable. However, nonequivalent comparison groups used in time series provide more reliable evidence on the causal effects of a policy. Such designs are referred to as *Control-Series* designs, and they attempt to control those aspects of history, maturation, and test-retest effects shared by the experimental and comparison groups.

Figure 3.7 illustrates these points for the Connecticut speeding crackdown, adding evidence from the fatality rates of neighboring states (the comparison group). To make the two series of comparable magnitude, Campbell presented the data as population-based fatality rates. The Control-Series design shows that downward trends were present in the neighboring states for 1955–1956 owing to history and maturation (weather, automotive safety devices, and so on). However, the data are also indicative of a general trend for Connecticut to rise relatively closer to the other states prior to 1955 and to drop steadily and more rapidly than other states from 1956 onward. With such evidence one can infer that the program had some effect over and above the regression artifact.

Another application of the Control-Series design is Franklin E. Zimring's evaluation of the impact of the federal Gun Control Act of 1968.[15] The major goals of the act were:

> (1) Eliminating the interstate traffic in firearms and ammunition that had previously frustrated state and local efforts to license, register, or restrict ownership of guns. (2) Denying access to firearms to certain congressionally defined groups, including minors, convicted felons, and persons who had been adjudicated as mental defectives or committed to mental institutions. (3) Ending the importation of all surplus military firearms and all other guns unless certified by the Secretary of the Treasury as "particularly suitable for . . . sporting purposes."[16]

Zimring assumed that if the act and its enforcement brought a

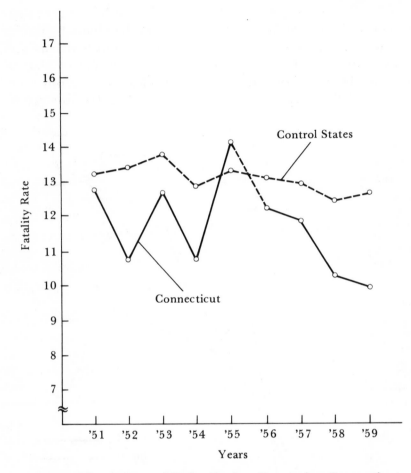

Figure 3.7   **A Control-Series Design Comparing Connecticut Traffic Fatalities with Those of Four Other States**

Source: Donald T. Campbell, "Reforms as Experiments," *American Psychologist*, 24 (April 1969), 419. Reprinted by permission.

reduction of interstate firearms traffic, this reduction would be evident in New York City and Boston, the principal cities in the two most restrictive handgun-licensing states in the United States, because out-of-state handguns are a higher proportion of total handguns in these two cities than in other metropolitan areas.

The number of violent crimes committed with handguns

served as a measure of the relative number of handguns in circulation. Figure 3.8 shows the number of handgun homicides reported by the police in New York and Boston and handgun homicide trends for fifty-seven cities with populations of 250,000 or more. In New York, handgun homicides grew steadily from 1966 to 1972, increasing three times as much as the fifty-seven–

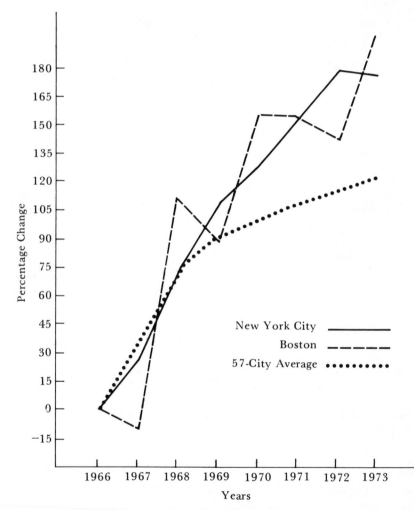

Figure 3.8   **Trends in Handgun Homicides by Years, New York City, Boston, and Fifty-seven–City Average**

Source: Franklin E. Zimring, "Firearms and Federal Law: The Gun Control Act of 1968," *Journal of Legal Studies,* 4 (January 1975), 177, Fig. 6. Reprinted by permission.

city average between 1969 and 1972. In Boston during 1969–1971, handgun homicides increased more than the fifty-seven–city average; there was a drop in 1972, followed by a large increase in 1973.

With the Control-Series design one can also compare the patterns of handgun violence in each city before and after introduction of the act. Such a comparison is essential for determining the effectiveness of the policy. The two cities show increases in handgun violence almost as great in the years following introduction of the act as in the years before. Moreover, both cities show more pronounced increases than the fifty-seven–city average during 1969–1973. Based on these and other related measures, Zimring concluded that if the hypothesis "that the rate at which handguns are introduced into an area is disproportionately reflected in rates of handgun violence is correct, the data suggest that the Gun Control Act of 1968 did not result in a palpable disruption of interstate handgun traffic."[17]

Control-Series designs are especially suited for evaluating policies that are not being applied simultaneously to all the units in a target population. Many policies and programs are matters of state and/or local jurisdiction rather than national. Such cases present opportunities for assessing the effectiveness of policies with Control-Series designs. Obviously, in such cases a major problem concerns the extent to which the experimental and comparison groups are equal in all significant factors. Units of analysis such as states and cities are far from similar in every detail. Consequently, the issue becomes one of assessing the extent to which "an imperfect match plausibly explains away the outcome without necessitating the assumption that [the policy] under study had an effect."[18] Similarities among the groups before implementation of a policy are most significant. Other things being equal, the validity of a causal inference on a policy's effectiveness will increase the less the likelihood for dissimilarities. Supplementary and/or circumstantial data can be of great value in establishing the extent to which the compared groups were similar before implementation of the policy.

But even with relatively unambiguous cases, the researcher has to examine the plausibility of alternative explanations. Factors such as changes in data-collection or record-keeping procedures in the experimental group, changes in the construction of the measuring instruments, and other changes unique to the experimental group might lead to incorrect inferences concerning the effectiveness of a policy. Analysis of supplementary data might help determine the plausibility of many of these rival interpretations.

Regression-Discontinuity Design

Given the reality of scarce resources, some policies and programs are not applied to all the cases in a target population but rather to a select number. This creates a situation in which more experimental cases are available than the number of those who are actually going to be inducted into a program. A similar condition obtains with pilot programs, in which a new program is tried out in a limited number of cases. For example, due to political considerations, lack of resources, and uncertainties about the effectiveness of the program, the New Jersey Negative Income Tax Experiment was carried out in only a few cities and not on the entire eligible target population.

The underlying idea of the Regression-Discontinuity design is that if a condition emerges in which there are more target units than program space, some of the eligible units can be used as a comparison group. Under such circumstances, as Campbell suggests, the most effective strategy would be the random assignment of target units occurring across the full range of eligibility.[19] By keeping records on the randomly selected comparison group, the researcher could later measure the target variables in both the experimental and comparison groups. In practice, however, randomization procedures are rarely employed. Instead, criteria such as "the most needy," "the most deserving," or "first come" are used. In such cases "tie-breaking" randomization procedures can be used to control for some plausible sources of invalidity.

The idea of tie-breaking experimentation evolved from the Thistlethwaite and Campbell experiments on the effects of receiving fellowships; that is, do academic awards exert an effect on later success in life?[20] The postulated relationship is illustrated in Figure 3.9, where pre-award ability and merit are measured on the horizontal axis and later achievement in life (e.g., earnings ten years after graduation) on the vertical. Students obtaining higher scores on the pre-award measure are most deserving and in fact receive

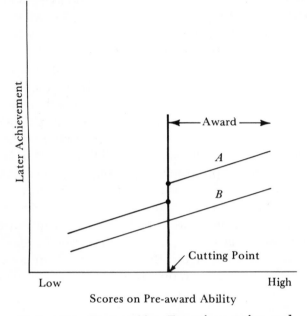

Figure 3.9   **Tie-breaking Experimentation and Regression Discontinuity**

the academic awards. These students also do better in later achievement. The problem is whether the award has a causal effect since the higher-ability students would generally do better in later achievement anyway.

In this case full randomization of the awards is impossible in light of the policy to reward ability and merit. Nevertheless, Campbell suggests, "It might be possible to take a narrow band of ability at the cutting point, to regard all these persons as tied, and to assign half of them to awards, half to no awards, by means of tie-breaking randomization."[21] If the tie-breakers were to show an effect, there should be an abrupt discontinuity in the regression line. The discontinued regression line *A* in Figure 3.9 demonstrates a case in which higher preprogram scores would have led to higher postprogram scores even without application of the program, and in which there is in addition a substantial program effect. The regression line *B* in this figure shows a case in which the program has no effect.

The essential requirement for a Regression-Discontinuity design is a sharp cutoff point in the eligibility criterion. Another requirement is that there be a sufficient number of cases. One way to maximize the number of subjects who are tied at the cutoff score is to use relatively large class intervals within which scores would be regarded as equal. For example, in the New Jersey Negative Income Tax Experiment, a $50 per month interval would yield a larger number of ties than would, say, a $10 per month interval. The third requirement for the application of the Regression-Discontinuity design is that the eligibility criterion be quantified. For some public programs a quantitative criterion is already included among several eligibility criteria—for instance, family income in the New Jersey Experiment or in the Neighborhood Youth Corps and scores on several tests in Head Start. Other programs, however, lack any quantitative criterion for determining eligibility. In such cases, if the Regression-Discontinuity design is to be applied, ranking or rating procedures can be used. Such procedures are examined in chapter four.

Combined Designs

The previous sections focused on the weakest and the strongest of the many possible quasi-experimental designs.[22] The stronger designs control in more effective ways for more intrinsic factors (for example, history, maturation, regression artifacts) that might invalidate inferences concerning the causal effects of policies. If the measurement procedures do not vary from one point of measurement to the next, instrument decay can also be ruled out as a source of invalidity. The weakest quasi-experimental designs introduce a greater measure of ambiguity of inference. Nevertheless, they are better suited for policy evaluation research than are pre-experimental designs. Recently, Robert F. Boruch, among others, has systematically elaborated possibilities for combining two or more designs in a single evaluation study. Such an approach involves "nesting randomized experiments in a larger framework of quasi-experimental or completely nonquantitative evaluation."[23]

Perhaps one of the most instructive investigations that combined designs to assess causal effects is that of the Salk vaccine—a preventive medication for paralytic poliomyelitis first experimented with in 1954.[24] In the initial design the idea was to give

the vaccine only to those second graders whose parents volun-
teered them for study and not to give it to first and third graders.
Presumably the comparison of results for the experimental group
and the comparison groups would be indicative of the vaccine's
effectiveness. Such a research design was most vulnerable, however, because polio occurred more frequently in more-sanitary
neighborhoods than in unsanitary ones, and the more-sanitary
neighborhoods are associated with higher socioeconomic status.
People of higher socioeconomic status tend to volunteer more than
people of lower socioeconomic status. Consequently, it could have
been expected that more volunteers in the second grade would
have been prone to have the disease in the first place than second
graders in general and the average of the first and third graders.
This bias could have invalidated the comparison. Furthermore, if
only second graders were vaccinated, physicians might have sus-
pected that some of them had caught paralytic polio because of
exposure to the vaccine itself, so that there might have been significant frequency differences in diagnoses in the volunteer and
nonvolunteer groups.

Realizing these problems, some state public health officials recommended a controlled field experiment that randomized the
vaccine among volunteers from all grade groups. Half the volunteers received the vaccine and half a salt-water injection (placebo),
so that the "blindness" of the diagnoses could be protected and
physicians could be shielded from their expectations for the outcome in making a diagnosis. In other words, the self-selection
source of invalidity would be balanced between the vaccinated and
unvaccinated groups of volunteers.

Some states applied the original design and others the randomized controlled design. The results of the latter conclusively showed
a reduction in the paralytic polio rate from about 57 per 100,000
among the comparison groups to about 16 per 100,000 in the
experimental group. In the states where only the second-grade
volunteers were vaccinated, the experimental group had about the
same rate (17 per 100,000) as those vaccinated in the placebo
comparison neighborhoods. The expected bias of an increased
rate for volunteers compared with nonvolunteers appeared among
the whole group. Among the placebo comparisons, the volunteers
who were not vaccinated had the highest rate (57 per 100,000),

and those who declined to volunteer had about 36 per 100,000. In the states using the initial nonexperimental design, the first and third graders, who were not asked to volunteer and were not vaccinated, had a rate between the two extremes, 46 per 100,000.

In the Salk vaccine investigation, the two research designs were used simultaneously, and they supported each other. However, in many other situations the use of a quasi-experimental design alone does not provide sufficient confidence in the results. Moreover, when complex policies are to be evaluated, one or more of the major components of such policies can frequently be studied experimentally and the remaining components with quasi-experimental designs:

> There is often ample justification for the view that components of a complex program (rather than the total program) should be tested using randomized experiments. The component evaluations can often be engineered nicely into a larger quasi-experimental framework for assessment. And when conducted properly, they can help to identify how well microelements of a social program are working, even if political or ethical constraints prevent randomized tests of macroelements or of the complete program.[25]

Component experimentation is also helpful when larger and complex programs are being implemented without prior evidence but with strong conviction that the program is effective. In such cases the researcher can examine those components of the program about which there is some doubt as to their effectiveness.

To exemplify more concretely the idea of experiments within quasi-experimental designs, recall that the Regression-Discontinuity design involves situations in which individuals or other units of analysis are selected for a program on the basis of eligibility; if the program has an effect, a sharp discontinuity in the regression line will emerge. To establish more systematic evidence of a program's effect for specified ranges of eligibility, randomized experiments can be performed within those ranges, or at other intervals along the eligibility continuum, as illustrated in Figure 3.10.[26]

Another type of coupling between experimental and quasi-experimental designs involves quasi-experiments within experiments. Possibilities for such combinations arise when randomization of one type of unit of analysis is impossible or impractical, but

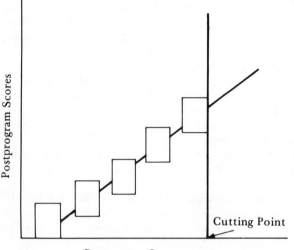

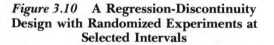

Figure 3.10   **A Regression-Discontinuity Design with Randomized Experiments at Selected Intervals**

randomization of a group of units can be achieved. For example, it might not be feasible to assign individuals randomly to a program within a neighborhood; it might be possible, however, to identify eligible districts and then to assign eligible neighborhoods to the program randomly. Such a procedure permits construction of a controlled experiment for the organizational units and a quasi-experiment for the individuals residing in the selected neighborhoods.

NOTES

1. This account draws upon Walter Williams, *Social Policy Research and Analysis: The Experience in the Federal Social Agencies* (New York: Elsevier, 1971); and Walter Williams and John W. Evans, "The Politics of Evaluation: The Case of Head Start," *Annals of the American Academy of Political and Social Science,* 385 (September 5, 1969), 118–132.
2. The Head Start program was subsequently evaluated with different research designs, which are discussed in later sections.

3. Donald T. Campbell, "Reforms as Experiments," *American Psychologist*, 24 (April 1969), 411.
4. Donald T. Campbell and Albert Erlebacher, "How Regression Artifacts in Quasi-Experimental Evaluations Can Mistakenly Make Compensatory Education Look Harmful," in Jerome Hellmuth, ed., *Compensatory Education: A National Debate*, Vol. III of *The Disadvantaged Child* (New York: Brunner/ Mazel, 1970), pp. 185–210.
5. Some refer to this group as a "simulated control group." See, for example, Fred N. Kerlinger, *Foundations of Behavioral Research*, 2nd ed. (New York: Holt, Rinehart & Winston, 1973), p. 321.
6. Categoric group members merely share some attribute that assigns them to an identifiable category.
7. For this and other possible artifacts in measurement, see Derek L. Philips, *Knowledge from What?* (Chicago: Rand McNally, 1971), especially pp. 21–49.
8. Jim C. Nunnally, "The Study of Change in Evaluation Research: Principles Concerning Measurement, Experimental Designs, and Analysis," in Elmer L. Struening and Marcia Guttentag, eds., *Handbook of Evaluation Research*, I (Beverly Hills, Calif.: Sage, 1975), p. 131.
9. The following account draws on Herbert I. Weisberg, *Short Term Cognitive Effects of Head Start Programs: A Report on the Third Year of Planned Variation—1971–1972* (Cambridge, Mass.: Huron Institute, September 1973).
10. Donald T. Campbell and Julian C. Stanley, *Experimental and Quasi-Experimental Designs for Research* (Chicago: Rand McNally, 1966), p. 39.
11. Campbell, "Reforms as Experiments"; and Henry W. Riecken and Robert F. Boruch, eds., *Social Experimentation: A Method for Planning and Evaluating Social Intervention* (New York: Academic Press, 1974), pp. 101–103.
12. Campbell, "Reforms as Experiments," p. 413.
13. Ibid.
14. Statistical techniques for characterizing time series are presented in chapter five.
15. Franklin E. Zimring, "Firearms and Federal Law: The Gun Control Act of 1968," *Journal of Legal Studies*, 4 (January 1975), 133–198.
16. Ibid., p. 149.
17. Ibid., p. 180.
18. Riecken and Boruch, eds., *Social Experimentation*, p. 99.
19. Campbell, "Reforms as Experiments," p. 419.
20. Donald L. Thistlethwaite and Donald T. Campbell, "Regression-Discontinuity Analysis: An Alternative to the Ex Post Facto Experiment," *Journal of Educational Psychology*, 51 (December 1960), 309–317.
21. Campbell, "Reforms as Experiments," p. 420.
22. For other types of quasi-experimental designs, see James A. Caporaso and Leslie L. Roos, Jr., eds., *Quasi-Experimental Approaches: Testing Theory and Evaluating Policy* (Evanston, Ill.: Northwestern University Press, 1973).
23. Robert F. Boruch, "Coupling Randomized Experiments and Approximations to Experiments in Social Program Evaluation," in Ilene N. Bernstein,

ed., *Validity Issues in Evaluative Research,* Sage Contemporary Social Science Issues, XXIII (Beverly Hills, Calif.: Sage, 1976), p. 43.

24. The following account leans on Paul Meier, "The Biggest Public Health Experiment Ever: The 1954 Field Trial of the Salk Poliomyelitis Vaccine," in Judith M. Tamur et al., eds., *Statistics: A Guide to the Unknown* (San Francisco: Holden-Day, 1972), pp. 2–13; and K. A. Brownlee, "Statistics of the 1954 Polio Vaccine Trials," *Journal of the American Statistical Association,* 50 (1955), 1005–1013.

25. Boruch, "Coupling Randomized Experiments," p. 43.

26. Ibid., pp. 47–48.

Chapter Four
Measurement and Social Indicators

Once an impact model is constructed and an appropriate research design is developed, a decision must be made about what kinds of data are to be collected and how they are to be analyzed. Data for policy evaluation research can be obtained from various sources and by various methods; some of the major sources are considered in the following section. Next, the idea of "social indicators" is introduced. These are quantitative descriptions of social, economic, and political conditions expressed in time series. Such indicators can serve as supplementary evidence when a research design fails to control for sources of invalidity such as history or maturation. By providing an overall description of societal processes and of changes that take place in society, social indicators are significant not only for policy evaluation but also for policy decisions.

Ultimately, all data must be subjected to some sort of analysis. This is achieved by measurement. The principles of measurement and some basic methods for constructing measures are discussed in the third and fourth sections. The last section focuses on techniques for assessing the quality of data—that is, their validity and reliability.

SOURCES OF DATA

Sources of data for testing impact models can be generally classified as obtrusive or unobtrusive. Obtrusive data-collection methods refer to procedures in which data are collected through some form of direct solicitation and in which program personnel and participants are aware that the research is going on. The more commonly used obtrusive methods are interviews, questionnaires, and various forms of observation. Unobtrusive methods of data collection are procedures that remove the investigator from the phenomenon being researched. For example, documents such as minutes of board meetings or newspaper accounts represent unobtrusive data because the conditions leading to their generation are not influenced by the behavior and the expectations of the researcher.[1] The more commonly used obtrusive and unobtrusive methods will be briefly described here.

Interviews

The interview is a face-to-face interpersonal role situation in which an interviewer asks the respondent questions designed to obtain answers pertinent to the evaluation study. The questions, their wording, and their sequence define the extent to which the interview is structured.

The most structured form of interview is the *schedule-structured interview,* in which the questions, their wording, and their sequence are fixed and are identical for every respondent. This is done to make sure that when variations appear among the respondents, they can be attributed to actual differences among them and not to variations in the interview. The researcher attempts to reduce the risk that changes in the wording of questions, for instance, might elicit differences in responses.

A second form of interviewing is the *focused interview.* This form has four distinct features: (1) it is conducted with respondents known to have been involved in a particular program; (2) it refers to situations that have been analyzed prior to the interview; (3) it proceeds on the basis of an interview guide that specifies topics related directly to the study; and (4) it is focused on the subjective experiences involved in the situations under study. Respondents are given considerable liberty in expressing their definitions of the situation that is presented by the interviewer. The focused interview makes it possible to probe and obtain details such as personal reactions and specific emotions.

The least structured form of interview is the *nondirective interview.* Here no prespecified set of questions is employed, nor are the questions asked in a specified order, and no schedule is used. With little or no direction from the interviewer, respondents are encouraged to relate their experiences, to describe whatever events seem significant to them, to provide their own definitions of their situations, and to reveal their opinions as they see fit.

Obviously, if the researcher is concerned with ascertaining the respondents' meanings and definitions, the less structured interviews are more suitable. If, however, the research objective is to collect the same kind of information from all respondents, a schedule-structured interview is necessary.[2]

Questionnaires

Questionnaires are another method of data collection widely used in evaluation research to obtain factual and attitudinal data. The questions must be worded so that they are comprehended by the respondent in the manner that the researcher intends. If the target population is individuals from all walks of life, the wording of the questions should be understandable by the average eighth grader. Furthermore, words that are subject to a wide variety of interpretations should either be avoided or qualified by specifying their frame of reference.

Questions in a questionnaire can be either open-ended or fixed-alternative. In a fixed-alternative question, respondents are offered a set of answers from which they are asked to choose one that most closely represents their views. For example, to measure the effectiveness of a manpower retraining program, participants could be asked the following fixed-alternative question:

"To what extent did the program help you to find your present job?"

☐ To a very great extent
☐ To a great extent
☐ Little
☐ Not at all
☐ Don't know

Fixed-alternative questions are easy to ask and quick to answer; they require no writing by either respondent or interviewer, and their analysis is straightforward. Their major drawback is that they may introduce bias, either by forcing respondents to choose from given alternatives, or by making respondents think of alternatives that might not have occurred to them.

Open-ended questions are not followed by any kind of choice, and the respondents' answers are recorded in full. The virtue of open-ended questions is that they do not force respondents to adapt to preconceived answers; they can express their thoughts freely, spontaneously, and in their own language. However, open-ended questions are difficult to answer and still more difficult to analyze. The researcher has to design a coding frame to classify the various answers; in the process, the details of the information provided by the respondent might get lost.

Another consideration in constructing questionnaires involves leading questions—that is, questions phrased in such a manner that it appears to the respondent that the interviewer expects a certain answer. For instance, a question designed to elicit attitudes toward a given program might read: "How do you feel about the program?" The same question phrased in a leading form might read: "You wouldn't say that you were in favor of the program, would you?" A more subtle form of a leading question might be: "Would you say that you are not in favor of the program?" This last question makes it easier for respondents to answer "yes" than "no." In answering "yes" they are agreeing with the language of the question and are not contradicting the interviewer. Unless leading questions serve a definite research purpose, they should be avoided if undistorted responses are wanted.

The questions that comprise the questionnaire may be presented to the respondents at random or in a systematic way. Two general patterns of questions have been found to be most appropriate for motivating respondents to cooperate with the interviewer: the funnel sequence and the inverted funnel sequence. In the funnel sequence, each successive question is related to the previous question and has a progressively narrower scope. By asking the broadest questions first, the interviewer can avoid imposing a frame of reference before obtaining the respondent's perspective. Broader questions should also be pursued first when the objective of the interview is to discover unanticipated responses. In the inverted funnel sequence, narrower questions are followed by broader ones. When the topic of the questionnaire does not strongly motivate the respondent to communicate, it may be helpful to begin with the narrower questions, which are easier to answer, while reserving the broader (and more difficult) ones until later.[3]

Observation

The principal virtue of observation is its directness; it makes possible the study of behavior as it occurs. This permits the generation of firsthand data that are uncontaminated by factors standing between the researcher and the object of research. For example, when people are asked to report their past behavior, distortions in recall may significantly contaminate the data, but the extent to which the individual is capable of remembering things has no effect on data collected through observation.

Observation takes many forms. It includes the most casual experiences as well as the most sophisticated laboratory devices. It may take place in a natural setting or in a contrived environment such as the laboratory. Laboratory observation involves the introduction of conditions in a controlled environment (laboratory) that simulates certain features of the natural environment. It allows the construction of a situation with closely supervised manipulation of one or more independent variables at a time in order to observe the effects produced. Field observation, on the other hand, as the term implies, is a study in a natural situation. The research design issues and implementation problems involved with these two forms of observation were discussed in chapter two.[4]

Documents

Documents such as minutes of board meetings, budget proposals, mass-media accounts, and archival records in general are a major source of unobtrusive data. A large amount of such data is readily available to the public. Some of these records have been compiled specifically for purposes of research, whereas others have been prepared for more general consumption. Documents have been used both as a primary source of data and to supplement and cross-validate data collected by other methods. For example, Robert C. Angell used city budgets as a primary source of data to investigate the "moral integration" of cities. He constructed a "welfare effort index" by computing local per capita expenditures for welfare; the index was then combined with a "crime index" based on data from the Federal Bureau of Investigation to get an "integration index."[5]

A more recent development in the utilization of documents for policy evaluation research is found in public health programs, where medical records are being systematically used to describe and evaluate services to individuals and groups. Emphasis is being placed on the complex of agencies, facilities, and staff which together comprise a system of service for residents of defined geographical areas. Data are being collected concerning three major areas: (1) individual patients—admission information, during-services information, information at conclusion of service, and after-service information; (2) monitor programs—dealing with general questions such as what the facility is doing and how the system is working, and specific questions such as how many patients were admitted to the facility and what the dollar costs were; (3) program development—concerned with problems such as what the facility catchment area is like in general and what the mental health needs of the area are.[6]

Data Banks

With the development of computers, considerable efforts have been devoted to the establishment and maintenance of data banks. Storage systems on the national level attempt to pool data and research findings of large numbers of local and regional studies on the same subjects and problems. Storage systems at the state or regional level attempt to consolidate studies undertaken on a variety of problems so that the data can be pooled. Such data can be used for comparative purposes, replications, and as supplementary evidence for both experimental and quasi-experimental designs.[7] Relatedly, some information-retrieval systems provide references and information already reported in the research literature. In fields such as health and poverty, computer-based information services supply various sorts of descriptive data. For example, the system at the National Library of Medicine provides a dictionary-type listing of various topics, and one can request materials listed on an item or combination of items in the dictionary. These and other technological developments, growing societal complexities, and shared concerns over future directions led to the emergence of social-indicator systems.

SOCIAL INDICATORS

The term *social indicators* refers to quantitative descriptions and analyses of societal conditions and trends. Operationally, this means that social indicators are time series that allow both comparisons over an extended period and disaggregation* by other relevant attributes.[8] As such, social indicators can aid in assessing the effectiveness of policies, provide insights into the state of the nation, and may "ultimately make possible a better evaluation of what public programs are accomplishing."[9] Implicit in this aim is the assumption that a reliable system of social indicators will provide the data base necessary for the establishment of a social accounting system capable of recording the gains that result from policies and programs as well as their social costs.[10]

Social indicators can be classified into three general types: descriptive, output descriptive, and analytic.[11] These three types of indicators are not mutually exclusive; they feed back into each other, and each shares the attributes of time-series data and the possibility for disaggregation.

Descriptive indicators are general measures of social conditions and the changes that take place in the society. For example, time series of the distributions of education and income among minority groups are descriptive indicators.

Output descriptive indicators are measures of the end products of social processes and are intended for direct use in policy decisions. Three considerations have been proposed to be relevant when considering whether to cover a substantive area by output descriptive indicators:

1. Acknowledged social goals—"Every end-state which can be appropriately described as a national goal ought to be represented by one or more social indicators."[12] For instance, in the U.S. Department of Health, Education, and Welfare publication *To-*

---

* Disaggregation of an indicator means separation or breakdown of an indicator into its relevant component parts—for example, region, socioeconomic status, age, ethnicity, education.

ward a Social Report, some of the areas that meet this description are:

Health and Illness: Are We Becoming Healthier?
Social Mobility: How Much Opportunity Is There?
Income and Poverty: Are We Better Off? [13]

2. Emerging societal goals—for each area covered by output descriptive indicators, there might be emerging goals as well as acknowledged goals.

3. Potential for change—since the major purpose of output descriptive indicators is social improvement, priority should be given to those indicators which promise to enhance the realization of intended changes. [14]

The third type of social indicator, analytic indicators, serve as components of conceptual models of the social processes that result in the values of the output descriptive indicators. For example, estimates of the differences in income distribution between blacks and whites derived from an explicit model of the society's stratification structure are analytic indicators.

Sources of Information

Research work on social indicators has evolved around the following categories of data: (1) available data, (2) replication of baseline studies, (3) demographic and social accounting, and (4) subjective measures of the quality of life.

Available Data   The Census Bureau's *Current Population Reports* include information on changes in the economic and social conditions of minority groups, youth, and city populations. Such information describes social trends and has been used fruitfully for various purposes in the literature on social indicators. More recently, the National Center for Health Statistics has published reports on topics such as "Age Patterns in Medical Care, Illness, and Disability" and "Health Characteristics of Low-Income Persons." These reports were organized with the purpose of describing significant social trends, and as such they have been valuable for the study of social change. These documents, however, form the exception. In general, as Robert Park and Eleanor B. Sheldon point out, the rule has been that "The Federal statistical establishment annually disgorges immense amounts of social data, only a fraction of which gets distilled as knowledge about social change."[15] Although federal statistical reports pay much attention to how the data were compiled, they fail to adhere to accepted analytical techniques and methods of data presentation. For many areas of interest the data are available; what is missing is "a mandate and support for the development of analytical measures of major social trends comparable to the emphasis given to economic trends."[16]

Replication of Baseline Studies   Another approach to the development of social indicators has been through what Otis Dudley Duncan has called the "replication of baseline studies" to measure societal change. In *Toward Social Reporting: Next Steps*, Duncan has suggested that when such replications are done properly, differences between the original and the new findings would represent quite reliable estimates of the direction and extent of societal change over the intervening period.[17] The Detroit Area Study (DAS) established at the University of Michigan in 1951 exemplifies this approach.[18]

The chief objectives of DAS have been to provide reliable data on the Greater Detroit community and to serve as a resource for basic research. Surveys have been conducted annually since 1951–1952 on various topics including racial prejudice, changes in child-rearing practices, the prestige of public employment, and annual changes in family income. In 1971 DAS focused on measuring change over time. The major problem was to decide which previous studies were most promising as sources of baseline measurements. Two considerations were dominant. First, "We wanted the span of time to be as great as possible, on the theory that the measurement of trend, if only two observations are available, is more reliable if these observations are widely spaced than if they are close together."[19] The second consideration was that the baseline pertain to a cross-section population. Employing these criteria, researchers selected eight surveys as baseline measurements. From these, the 1971 survey included questions for replication believed to be helpful in developing standard social indicators that would warrant periodic replication in the future and for which favorable evidence concerning their validity was available. The survey covered five broad topics: marriage and family; age and sex roles;

civics and public affairs; participation and alienation; religion, class, and race.

Demographic and Social Accounting   This approach is grounded on comprehensive mathematical models of various aspects of the society as its starting point. For example, Richard Stone has elaborated a system of demographic accounts and demographic models based on the application of input-output analysis. These models describe the processes by which people move into and out of the population under study. Stone applied such models to problems in education, to referrals in systems of medical care, and to recruitment and promotion in formal organizations.[20]

James S. Coleman employed Stone's scheme as a basis for hypothetical experimentation on the effects of social processes. The model he developed describes the entry of persons into a system of occupations and their movement from one occupation to another while they are in that system. The model constitutes "an accounting scheme for tracing members of a population's birth into and progression through a system of states . . . Certain assumptions, such as constancy of the transition matrix . . . make the model more than descriptive, and able to make predictions about future distributions in the system."[21]

Subjective Measures of the Quality of Life   In general, a distinction is made between "objective" and "subjective" dimensions of life. By objective is meant environmental conditions such as housing, recreational resources, pollution; and attributes of individuals such as health, educational achievement, family stability, and the like. The subjective dimension, on the other hand, refers to aspects of personal experience such as satisfactions, aspirations, and frustrations. Indeed, it is assumed that social well-being depends jointly on these two dimensions.

Current research on subjective indicators of the quality of life includes attempts to measure levels of satisfaction and sources of satisfaction in several domains of life such as housing, community, nation, friends, family, health, job, leisure-time activities, and financial status.[22] In addition to general surveys of life satisfaction, research is being conducted with specific reference to the relationship between economic behavior and subjective well-being. Studies have been developed to measure workers' subjective evaluations of the working environment, including such areas as earnings, time required to get to work, job enrichment, behavior of supervisors, promotion histories, and the like.[23] This research is an attempt to assess the impact that subjective evaluation of the working environment has on an individual's general feelings and his or her attitudes toward work.[24]

MEASUREMENT SCALES

Data must be subjected to analysis. The transformation of all sorts of information into ordered data amenable to quantitative analysis is achieved through measurement. Measurement serves three significant purposes. First, it permits the utilization of powerful mathematical and statistical analyses; the latter, in turn, reveal information and insights that cannot be obtained otherwise. Second, quantification allows for precision and makes it possible to report results in finer detail than would be practicable with qualitative judgments; for example, one could tell *how* effective a policy or a public program is. Last, when measurement procedures are made public and are replicated, a greater degree of credibility is attained.

Essentially, measurement refers to the assignment of numbers to objects, properties (and their indicators), or events according to a set of rules.[25] A precise formulation of the rules provides an operational definition of what it is that is being measured. That is, operational definitions tie measurement to reality. The crucial question to be answered in measurement is whether the assigned numerical system is similar in structure to the structure of the entities that are being measured. In other words, are the two structures isomorphic? Researchers, as Sidney Siegel, among others, suggests, must always be alert to the fact that in order for them to be able to make "certain operations with numbers that have been assigned to observations, the structure of [their] method of mapping numbers to observations must be isomorphic to some numerical structure which includes these operations."[26] If two systems are isomorphic, their structures are the same in the relations and operations they allow for. Thus, if we assign numbers to objects and then manipulate these numbers, say by adding them, we are implying that the structure of this measurement is isomorphic to the numerical structure known as arithmetic.

The requirement of isomorphism between numerical systems and observable properties or their indicators leads to a distinction among different ways of measuring—that is, to three distinct types of measurement scales: nominal, ordinal, and interval.

Nominal Scales

The weakest level of measurement is attained with nominal scales. At this level, numbers or other symbols are used to classify objects, properties, events, or their indicators. These numbers or symbols constitute a nominal, or a classificatory, scale. By means of the symbols 1 and 2, for instance, it is possible to classify a given population into males and females, with 1 representing males and 2 standing for females. The same population can be classified by education: primary-school graduates might be represented by the numeral 6, high-school graduates by 7, and college graduates by 8. In the first case, the population was classified into two categories; in the second, into three. As a rule, when a set of properties can be classified into categories that are exhaustive (i.e., that include all objects) and mutually exclusive (i.e., with no case in more than one category), and when each category is represented by a different symbol, a nominal scale is attained.

Mathematically, the basic property of the nominal scale is that the properties of objects in one category are equal to each other but not to anything else. The logical properties of equivalence are reflexivity, symmetry, and transitivity. Reflexivity implies that every object in one of the categories is equal to itself; for example, $a = a$ in the "primary-school graduates" category. Symmetry is defined as the relationship when if $a = b$ then $b = a$. Transitivity is the relationship when if $a = b$ and $b = c$, then $a = c$. These three logical relations are operative among objects within the same category but not necessarily between categories. For instance, these relations will apply to all persons classified as "females" but not between "females" and "males." With nominal scales, the classification of objects may be equally well represented by any set of symbols. The symbols may also be interchanged without altering any information if this is done consistently and completely.

Ordinal Scales

Many properties are not only classifiable but also exhibit patterns of relations. Typical relations are "higher," "greater," "more desired," "more difficult," and so on. Such relations may be designated by the symbol ($>$), which means "greater than." For instance, the statement that policy A is more effective than policy B but less so than policy C can be expressed as $C > A > B$. In general, if (in addition to equivalence) the relation $>$ or $<$ ("less than") holds for all pairs of objects engendering a complete rank ordering of objects, an ordinal scale is attained. Consider a property such as "health status." It can be operationalized in terms of states of disability. Individuals can be classified into one of the five categories: "very sick," "sick," "early sick," "worried well," "well." The equivalence relation holds among members of the same category, whereas the $>$ relation holds between any pair of categories.

The $>$ relation is irreflexive, asymmetrical, and transitive. Irreflexivity is a logical property wherein it is not true that for any a, $a > a$. Asymmetry means that if $a > b$, then $b \not> a$. Transitivity means that if $a > b$, and $b > c$, then $a > c$. In other words, if a property such as "effectiveness" is measured on the ordinal level, one can infer that if policy A is more effective than policy B, and if B is more effective than C, then A is more effective than C, and that the $>$ relation is maintained with regard to all the policies in the set.

Ordinal scales are unique up to a monotonic transformation; that is, any order-preserving transformation does not change the information obtained. It does not matter what numbers one assigns to a pair of objects or to a category of objects so long as one is consistent. It is a matter of convenience whether to use lower numbers for the "more preferred" states, although we do usually refer to excellent performance as "first class" and to progressively inferior performances as "second class" and "third class." The numbers assigned to ranked objects are called *rank values*. Rank values are assigned to objects according to the following rule: the greatest (or the smallest) object is assigned 1; the next in size, 2;

the third in size, 3; and so on to the smallest (or greatest) object, which is assigned the last number in a given series.

Interval Scales

If in addition to being able to order objects or their indicators in terms of the > relation, one also knows the exact distance between each of the objects and this distance is constant, then an interval scale is obtained. In addition to saying that one object is greater than another, one can also specify by how many units the former is greater than the latter. To make these quantitative comparisons, one must have a unit of measurement. Properties such as height, temperature, time, income, intelligence quotient, and air pollution are measured at the interval level. An interval scale, then, is characterized by a common and constant unit of measurement that assigns a real number to all pairs of objects in the ordered set. In this kind of measurement, the ratio of any two intervals (distances) is independent of the unit of measurement.

The structure of the interval level of measurement is such that the differences between objects are isomorphic to the structure of arithmetic. Numbers may be assigned to the positions of the objects so that the operations of arithmetic may be meaningfully executed on the differences between these numbers. The following formal properties are operative with interval scales:

Uniqueness: if a and b stand for real numbers, then $a + b$ and $a \times b$ each represent one—and only one—real number.

Symmetry: if $a = b$, then $b = a$.

Commutation: if a and b denote real numbers, then $a + b = b + a$, and $ab = ba$.

Substitution: if $a = b$ and $a + c = d$, then $b + c = d$; and if $a = b$ and $ac = d$, then $bc = d$.

Association: if a, b, and c stand for real numbers, then $(a + b) + c = a + (b + c)$, and $(ab)c = a(bc)$.

Any change in the numbers assigned to the objects measured must preserve not only the ordering of objects but also the relative differences between the objects. In more formal language, interval scales are unique up to a linear transformation. Thus, the information obtained with interval scales is not affected if each number is multiplied by a positive constant and then a constant is added to this product.[27]

Scale Properties

The three scales of measurement themselves form a cumulative scale. That is, an ordinal scale possesses all the properties of a nominal scale plus ordinality; an interval scale has all the properties of both nominal and ordinal scales plus a unit of measurement. The cumulative nature of measurement scales implies that it is legitimate to drop back scales of measurement when analyzing and interpreting data. However, going up the scale of measurement from, say, an ordinal to an interval scale is a controversial issue since such transformations might violate the requirement for isomorphism.

Some methodologists contend that the power of the more sophisticated data-analysis methods compensates for problems that may arise from violating the requirement for isomorphism; that is, powerful statistics can legitimately be used with weak measurement scales.[28] Others have taken the position that when powerful statistics are applied to weaker measurement scales, the results should be taken as heuristic since "the ordinal level of measurement prohibits all but the weakest inferences concerning the fit between the data and the theoretical model formulated in terms of interval variables."[29] The position advanced in this book is that if the data are measured at an interval scale, procedures have to be formulated to check the consequences of the interval assumptions. For example, regression and path coefficients, discussed in the next two chapters, "are generally quite stable no matter what the interval scale, because appreciable distortion depends . . . on special coincidences between more than one kind of error."[30]

CONSTRUCTION OF MEASURES

To measure the variables contained in impact models, certain assumptions must be made concerning the correspondence between the structure of the data and scales of measurement. Furthermore, measures have to be constructed so that the data exhibit a systematic order that corresponds to the desired scale of measurement. Methods for constructing measures derive from scaling models. The purpose of any scaling model is to generate a continuum on which the properties of objects or their indicators are located. A common strategy in the development of a scaling model is to test for the presence of unidimensionality. For instance, participants in a public program can be asked either to agree or disagree with statements* concerning the effectiveness of the program. Agreement to each statement will represent positive evaluation; disagreement, negative evaluation. The sums of the agreements can constitute an ordering of individuals with respect to their evaluation of the program. A more rigorous technique to test for unidimensionality is the Guttman scalogram analysis, also termed Guttman scaling.

Guttman Scaling

The Guttman scaling technique was first developed by Louis Guttman during the early part of World War II to determine which of a series of attitude questions tapped the same underlying attitude.[31] Guttman suggested that if the items tap the same attitudinal dimension they can be arranged so that there will be an attitudinal continuum that indicates varying degrees of the underlying dimension. More explicitly, Guttman scales are unidimensional and cumulative.

Unidimensionality means that the component items measure movement toward or away from the same single underlying object. A cumulative scale implies that "the component items can be ordered by degree of difficulty and that the respondents who reply positively to a difficult item (question) will always respond positively to less difficult items and vice versa."[32] With, say, three items, this means that if a respondent agrees with item 3, he or she will also agree with items 2 and 1; and if another respondent agrees with item 2, he or she will also agree with item 1. The scale that would result from administering these three items to a group of respondents is illustrated in Table 4.1. This scale is unidimensional as well as cumulative: the items are unidimensionally ranked on a single underlying dimension, and the scale is cumulative in that none of the respondents has a − (disagreement) response before a + (agreement) response, or a + response after a − response. Thus, information on the position of any respondent's last positive re-

---

* The terms "statements," "questions," and "items" will be used interchangeably.

Table 4.1   A Hypothetical Perfect Guttman Scale*

	Items		
Scale Type	1	2	3
A	+	+	+
B	+	+	−
C	+	−	−
D	−	−	−

* + indicates agreement with the statement; − indicates disagreement.

sponse allows the prediction of all his or her other responses to the items.

In practice, a perfect Guttman scale is rarely obtainable. In most cases inconsistencies—a negative response before a positive one—are present. Consequently, it is necessary to establish a criterion for evaluating the unidimensional and the cumulative assumptions. Guttman developed the *coefficient of reproducibility* (CR) for this purpose:

$$CR = 1 - \frac{\text{inconsistencies}}{\text{total responses}} \tag{4.1}$$

A CR of .90 is the minimum standard for accepting a scale as unidimensional. In the hypothetical example shown in Table 4.2,

Table 4.2   Possible Guttman Scale Response Patterns

	Items		
Response Patterns	1	2	3
A	+	+	+
B	+	⊖	+
C	+	+	−
D	⊖	+	+
E	+	−	−
F	−	−	⊕
G	−	⊕	−
H	−	−	−

Table 4.3   **A Guttman Scale of Riot Severity**

Scale Type	% Cities (n = 75)	Items Reported	Scale Errors
8	4	No scale items	2
7	19	"Vandalism"	10
6	13	All of the above & "interference with firemen"	3
5	16	All of the above & "Looting"	3
4	13	All of the above & "Sniping"	7
3	7	All of the above & "called state police"	4
2	17	All of the above & "called National Guard"	11
1	11	All of the above & "law officer or civilian killed"	2
TOTAL	100%		42

Source: Jules J. Wanderer, "An Index of Riot Severity and Some Correlates," *American Journal of Sociology*, 74 (March 1969), 503, Table 1. Reprinted with permission.

the inconsistencies are circled; there are four inconsistencies and twenty-four possible responses, resulting in CR = .83 (1 − 4/24); that is, the scale is not unidimensional.[33]

One application of the Guttman scale is the riot-severity scale in American cities developed by Jules J. Wanderer. This is an eight-item scale with a CR of .93 (Table 4.3).

Likert Scales

Another common technique of scale construction is the Likert scale, or the "technique of summated rating." Five steps can be distinguished in the construction of a Likert scale. First, the researcher compiles a series of items expressive of the wide range of attitudes from extremely positive to extremely negative. Each item calls for checking one of five fixed-alternative expressions, such as "Strongly agree," "Agree," "Undecided," "Disagree," and "Strongly disagree."* In this five-point continuum, weights of 1, 2, 3, 4, 5, or 5, 4, 3, 2, 1 are assigned, the direction of weighting being determined by the favorableness or unfavorableness of the item.

* Occasionally three, four, six, or seven fixed-alternative expressions are used.

For example, to measure the role of alienation as a barrier to the utilization of preventive health services, the following question was included: "Sometimes I feel that life is not worth living." Respondents were asked to choose among one of the following five responses: (5) Strongly agree, (4) Agree, (3) Uncertain, (2) Disagree, (1) Strongly disagree.[34]

In the second step, a large number of respondents, selected randomly from the target population to be measured, are asked to check their attitudes on the list of items. Next, a total score for each respondent is calculated by summing the value of each item that is checked. Suppose a respondent checked "Strongly agree" in question 1 (score 5), "Agree" in question 2 (score 4), and "Strongly disagree" in the third question (score 1). His or her total score is $5 + 4 + 1 = 10$.

In the fourth step, the investigator has to determine the basis for the selection of items in the final scale. This can be done with "item analysis." Essentially, each item is subjected to a measurement of its ability to separate the "high" items on the attitude continuum from the "low" items. This is termed the discriminative power (DP) of the item. In calculating the DP, the scored responses to an item are summed and the scores placed in an array, usually from the lowest to the highest scores. In the final step, a comparison is made between the range above the upper quartile (Q_1) and that below the lower quartile (Q_4), and the DP is calculated as the difference between the weighted means of Q_1 and Q_4, as exemplified in Table 4.4. The DP index is computed for each of the items, and

Table 4.4 **DP Computing Table for One Item**

Group	Number in Group	1	2	3	4	5	Weighted Total*	Weighted Mean†	DP ($Q_1 - Q_4$)
High (top 25%)	9	0	1	2	3	3	35	3.89	
									2.00
Low (bottom 25%)	9	1	8	0	0	0	17	1.89	

* Weighted total = score × number checking that score.

† Weighted mean = $\dfrac{\text{weighted total}}{\text{number in group}}$.

those items with the largest DP values are selected for the final scale. These are the items that best discriminate among the expressed feelings toward the measured attitude.[35]

Multidimensional Scaling

The scaling techniques discussed so far are unidimensional. Sometimes, however, it becomes necessary to develop techniques of scaling that allow for two or more dimensions. The general purpose of multidimensional scaling is the mapping of relationships between variables in space along a number of dimensions. Thus, given a set of variables, the researcher attempts to align them in n-dimensional space in such a way that the most similar variables cluster together. Generally, the researcher seeks a representation of the lowest possible dimensionality consistent with the data. Such representation is more parsimonious in that it represents the same data by means of a small number of numerical parameters. Furthermore, to the extent that fewer parameters are delineated from the same data, each tends to be based upon a larger subset of the data.

Usually, for every two objects, i and j, in some set of n, the researcher is given data s_{ij} representing the proximity between them. He or she then looks for that configuration of n points in the Euclidean space of smallest possible dimension so that the resulting interpoint distances, d_{ij}, are monotonically related to the given proximity data. To find the optimum configuration of points, an explicit function is required.[36] Most of the functions that have been developed are based on the sum of squared discrepancies between the actually reconstructed distances and corresponding numbers that minimize this sum, subject to the constraint that the functions are monotonic with the corresponding data.[37]

Index Number Construction

Earlier, measurement was defined as the process of assigning numbers to objects or their indicators according to rules. The combination of two or more indicators yields a composite measure, usually referred to as an index. For instance, socioeconomic status is an index constructed by the combination of income, education, and occupational status. Another well-known type of index is the Consumer Price Index, a statistical measure of changes in retail prices.[38] The retail prices that make up the index are divided into eight major groups: food, housing, apparel, transportation, medical care, personal care, reading and recreation, and other goods and services. The approximately four hundred commodities and services that are included were selected as being representative of the price trends of subgroups of related items and include the cost of diverse commodities and services, such as rice, men's work gloves, women's wool suits, rent, mortgage interest, gasoline, and haircuts.

The four hundred commodities and services are collected from fifty urban areas selected to be representative of those city characteristics that affect the way in which families spend their money; factors such as city size, climate, population density, and income level are taken into consideration. Within each city, price quotations are obtained from those sources from which families of wage and salary workers purchase goods and services. For each item, the prices reported by the various sources are combined, with appropriate weights, to ascertain average price changes for the city. Index numbers are prepared monthly for the country and for each of five large cities, and quarterly for the other cities.

Four major problems are involved in constructing index numbers: definition of the purpose for which the index is being compiled; selection of sources of data; selection of base; and selection of methods of aggregation and weighting.

Definition of Purpose   Essential to the process of index number construction are the questions: What does one attempt to measure and how is the measure going to be used? Logically speaking, if A is an index of X, then A may be only one of several indices of X. Thus, some kind of supporting evidence is needed to make the case that the values of A correspond to the values of X. Most often, X is a broad concept like public welfare or health status. Such concepts consist of a complex combination of phenomena and are subject to differing interpretations. Accordingly, no single indicator will cover all the dimensions of a concept, and a number of indicators have to be developed. Each indicator, in turn, serves a specific purpose that must be explicated prior to construction of the index.

Selection of Data   Obtrusive and/or unobtrusive methods of data collection may be used to construct indices. Decisions as to which source of data to use depend on the purpose of the index and on the research design employed. As noted earlier, for some types of quasi-experimental designs both obtrusive and unobtrusive data are required. Under either circumstance, the investigator must ascertain that the data pertain strictly to the phenomenon being measured. This involves issues of validity and reliability, which will be discussed in the following section.

Selection of Base   For comparative purposes, indices are expressed in the form of a proportion, a percent, or a ratio. A proportion is defined as the frequency of observations in any given category (f_i) divided by the total number of observations (N), or f_i/N. A proportion may range from zero to 1. A proportion becomes a percent when multiplied by 100 $(f_i/N \times 100)$, and a percent, by definition, may range from zero to 100. A ratio expresses the relative magnitude of any two sets of frequencies, for instance, 6 to 21.

Table 4.5 reports the frequencies of selected criminal offenses in a New Jersey city by sources of official data. The one, Crime in New Jersey (CNJ), is compiled annually by the office of the state's attorney general. The other source was compiled from the municipal court dockets (MCD) in the city. For purposes of comparison and illustration, the data are expressed in the form of proportions and percents.[39]

Table 4.5   **Selected Offenses and Source of Information**

Selected Offenses	*CNJ*			*MCD*		
	f	PROPOR-TION	%	*f*	PROPOR-TION	%
Armed robbery	23	.04	4	0	.00	0
Robbery	17	.03	3	5	.01	1
Atrocious assault	13	.02	2	2	.007	.07
Simple assault	223	.40	40	250	.89	89
Break and entry	206	.37	37	1	.003	.3
Larceny	78	.14	14	24	.09	9
TOTAL	560	1.00	100	282	1.00	100

An examination of the table reveals a serious ambiguity in the meaning of crime data. There are differences in the amounts of officially recognized crime: CNJ reports more offenses than do court dockets. This is consistent with the fact that court dockets report information from a higher jurisdiction than does CNJ. CNJ reports offenses that are known to police, whereas court dockets report cases in which offenders have been identified, arrested, and booked on official complaints. Given that many offenses occur for which offenders are not apprehended, one would expect attrition of cases as these move upward through the levels of jurisdiction. However, the data for the "Simple assault" category are most problematic because it appears that municipal courts heard more cases of specific offenses than were known to the police in a city where the courts and the police shared jurisdiction. This indeed is improbable, and an index based on such data would be misleading.

Often it is necessary to shift the base of an index number series from one time period to another. For instance, shifting the base is necessary if index numbers of one series are to be meaningfully compared with those of another series. One method for shifting the base is to divide all the index numbers in the original series by the original value of the index number for the new base period and multiply by 100. This is illustrated with hypothetical data in Table 4.6. To obtain the new index number (with base 1969) for

Table 4.6   **Changing the Base of an Index Number**

Year	Values of Old Index (1973 = 100)	Values of New Index (1969 = 100)
1969	70	100.0
1970	80	114.3
1971	60	85.7
1972	95	135.7
1973	100	142.9
1974	115	164.3
1975	120	171.4
1976	118	168.6
1977	105	150.0

1969, we divide the original index number (with base 1973) for 1969 by 70 and then multiply by 100. This results in (70/70) × 100 = 100. The new index number for 1970 equals (80/70) × 100 = 114.3, and so on until the complete new series is obtained.[40]

Methods of Aggregation and Weighting   A common method for constructing index numbers is by computing aggregate values. The aggregates can be either simple or weighted, depending on the purpose of the index.

Simple Aggregates   Table 4.7 illustrates the construction of a simple aggregative price index. The prices of each commodity (C_i) in

Table 4.7   **Construction of Simple Aggregative Index Numbers (Hypothetical Data)***

Commodities	1973	1974	1975	1976	1977
C_1	$ 3.21	$ 4.14	$ 4.90	$ 5.80	$ 6.10
C_2	5.40	5.60	5.10	6.40	7.18
C_3	6.62	8.10	9.00	8.35	7.90
C_4	4.90	5.40	5.10	7.25	6.80
Aggregate value	$20.13	$23.24	$24.10	$27.80	$27.98
Index number†	100.00	115.45	119.72	138.10	139.00

* Prices are per unit.
† Percent of 1973.

any given year are added to give the index number for that year. As noted earlier, it is convenient to designate some year as a base, which is set equal to 100. In this example all the index numbers are expressed in the last row as a percentage of the 1973 number, obtained by dividing each of the numbers by the value in the base period ($20.13) and multiplying by 100. Symbolically,

$$PI = \Sigma p_n / \Sigma p_o \times 100 \qquad (4.2)$$

where *PI* stands for price index; *p* refers to the price of an individual commodity; *o* to the base period at which price changes are measured; and *n* refers to the given period that is being compared with the base. The formula for a particular year (for instance 1977, with 1973 being the base) is:

$$PI_{73,77} = \Sigma p_{77}/\Sigma p_{73} \times 100 \qquad (4.3)$$

Weighted Aggregates Simple aggregates may conceal the relative influence of each indicator of an index. To prevent such misrepresentation, weighted aggregates are often employed. To construct a weighted aggregative price index for the data in Table 4.7, a list of the quantities of the specified commodities is taken, and calculations are made to determine what this aggregate of goods is worth each year at current prices. This means that each unit price is multiplied by the number of units and the resulting values are summed for each period. Symbolically,

$$PI = \Sigma p_n q/\Sigma p_o q \times 100 \qquad (4.4)$$

where q represents the quantity of the commodity marketed, produced, or consumed; that is, the quantity weight, or multiplier. The procedure, using the quantities in 1973 as multipliers, is illustrated in Table 4.8. Since the total value changes while the components of the aggregate do not, these changes must be due to price changes. Thus the aggregative index numbers of price measure the changing value of a fixed aggregate of goods.[41]

Another illustration of index number construction is the Sellin and Wolfgang Index of Delinquency. To evaluate crime-control

Table 4.8 **Construction of Aggregative Index Numbers Weighted by Consumption in 1973**

Commodities	1973 Consump-tion*	Value of 1973 Quantity at Price of Specified Year				
		1973	1974	1975	1976	1977
C_1	800	$2,568	$3,312	$3,920	$4,640	$4,880
C_2	300	1,620	1,680	1,530	1,920	2,154
C_3	450	2,979	3,645	4,050	3,758	3,555
C_4	600	2,940	3,240	3,060	4,350	4,080
Aggregate value		$10,107	$11,877	$12,560	$14,668	$14,669
Index number†		100.0	117.5	124.3	145.1	145.1

* Hypothetical quantity units of consumption.
† Percent of 1973.

policies, at least three major types of information are required: data on the incidence of crimes; data on the response of the justice system; and data on the social and demographic characteristics of populations. With respect to incidence of crimes, a major problem is that offenses are varied in nature and magnitude. Some result in death, others inflict losses of property, and still others cause merely inconvenience. Yet the traditional way of comparing, say, one year's crime with another has been simply to count offenses, disregarding differences in content, shape, and size. Such unweighted indices are misleading. A police report that indicates merely an overall decline or increase in the total number of offenses committed may be misleading if there are significant changes in the type of offenses committed. For example, a small decline in "auto theft" but a large increase in "armed robbery" should lead to a decline in an unweighted crime index since reported auto thefts are usually much greater in absolute numbers than are reported armed robberies.[42]

In a genuine attempt to tackle this problem in the area of delinquency, Thorsten Sellin and Marvin E. Wolfgang developed a system of weighting by describing 141 carefully prepared accounts of different crimes to three samples of police officers, juvenile court judges, and college students.[43] The accounts of the different crimes included various combinations, such as death or hospitalization of the victim, type of weapon, and value of property stolen, damaged, or destroyed. For example, "The offender robs a person at gunpoint. The victim struggles and is shot to death"; "The offender forces open a cash register in a department store and steals five dollars"; "The offender smokes marijuana." Members of the samples were asked to rate each of these on a "category scale" and a "magnitude estimating scale," and their ratings were used to construct the weighting system. For example, a crime with the following "attributes" would be given the following number of points:

A house is forcibly entered	1
A person is murdered	26
The spouse receives minor injury	1
Between $251 and $2,000 are taken	2
TOTAL SCORE	30

With such an index, comparisons over time and between different communities can be carried out more meaningfully, taking into account the seriousness of the crimes committed.[44]

VALIDITY AND RELIABILITY

Previous sections were concerned with the logic and techniques for constructing measures. This section focuses on some central issues of validity and reliability. Essentially, validity is concerned with the question of whether one is measuring what one intends to measure. A measuring instrument is said to be valid if it does what it is intended to do. Reliability is an indication of the extent to which a measure contains variable errors. That is, it is assumed that any measure consists of a true component and an error component, and that the proportion of the amount of variation in the true component to the total variation estimates reliability. The idea of validity and some techniques for assessing the extent to which a given measure is valid are elaborated first.

Validity

The problem of validity arises in policy evaluation research because measurement, with few exceptions, is indirect. Under such circumstances, it is always necessary to provide evidence that a measure does in fact measure what it appears to measure. Validation always requires some kind of evidence, the nature of which depends on the type of validity. Three types of validity can be distinguished: predictive validity, content validity, and construct validity.

Predictive Validity   Predictive validity is at issue when the purpose is to use a measure to estimate a variable, the latter being referred to as the criterion. An example is a test used to select eligible children for Head Start. The test is useful only if it accurately estimates educational achievement in primary school. The criterion in this case could be grade-point average obtained over several years of schooling. After the criterion is obtained, the validation consists of correlating scores on the predictor test with scores on the criterion variable. The size of the correlation is an indication of the amount of validity.[45]

Two general points must be considered when employing the predictive validity technique. One relates to the validity of the criterion, and the other concerns the rationale that induces an investigator to use a measuring instrument and not the criterion itself; for example, why not measure grade-point averages directly? Regarding the second point, in some cases the criterion is technically difficult or too expensive to use, and in other cases investigators have to measure a property before they can make use of the criterion; for example, a child's potential has to be evaluated prior to his or her admission to a program.

Two common methods are used to determine the validity of the criterion. One method rests on agreement among researchers (intersubjective consensus) that a certain criterion is valid for evaluating a measure. A somewhat different method is to express the relationship between the instrument and the criterion in terms of the percentage of individuals (or other units of analysis) who would be correctly classified by the instrument according to their known attributes. Suppose one wishes to evaluate the validity of a measure or an indicator designed to measure access to medical care. If there are theoretically sound reasons for arguing that people in the lower class have less access than people in the middle class, the two groups can be compared as a check of predictive validity. In this case, social class serves as an indirect criterion to the predictive validity of the measure. If it is observed that persons in the lower class have as much access to medical care as persons in the middle class, the measure lacks predictive validity. On the other hand, a relatively high correlation between social class and access to medical care will tentatively validate the measure. However, one should be aware that a relatively high correlation is a necessary but not a sufficient condition of the predictive validity of a measure because the criterion (social class) may also be related to variables other than access to medical care. Thus, a criterion may at times be more useful for disvalidating than for validating a measure.

Content Validity   There are two varieties of content validity: face validity and sampling validity. Face validity rests on the researcher's subjective assessment of the validity of a measure. To make such assessments more credible, the researcher usually consults a number of specialists in the field. The extent of agreement among them serves as evidence of the face validity of the measure.

The primary concern of sample validity is whether a given population of situations, events, or behaviors is adequately sampled by the measure in question. That is, does the content of the measure adequately represent the content population of the variable being measured? The underlying assumptions of sampling validity are that every variable has a content population consisting of an infinite number of items and that a highly valid measure constitutes a representative sample of these items. In practice, problems arise with the definition of the content population, since this is, in principle, a theoretical rather than an empirical population.

Construct Validity   Construct validity involves relating a measure to an overall theoretical framework to determine whether the measure is tied to the concepts and theoretical assumptions that are being used. Lee J. Cronbach has observed that "Whenever a tester asks what a score means psychologically or what causes a person to get a certain test score, he is asking what concepts may properly be used to interpret the test performance."[46] The theoretical framework that a researcher has about the variable being measured leads him or her to postulate various kinds and degrees of relationships between the variable and other specified variables. To demonstrate construct validity of a measure, the researcher has to show that these relationships do in fact hold.

Lee Cronbach and Paul E. Meehl describe the logical process of construct validation.[47] First, a proposition that an indicator measures a certain variable, say variable A, is set forth; second, the proposition is inserted into the present theory of variable A; third, working through the theory, the researcher predicts other variables that should be correlated to the measure and variables that should exhibit no relation to variable A; finally, the researcher collects data on the basis of which the predicted relations are either confirmed or rejected. If the anticipated relations are confirmed, the measure is considered valid. On the other hand, if the predictions do not hold up, there are three possibilities: (1) the instrument does not measure variable A; (2) the theoretical framework that generated the prediction is incorrect; or (3) the research design failed to test the predictions properly. The researcher must then decide which of these three conditions has occurred, based on a careful reconstruction of each of the four steps that constitute the validation process.

Construct validation requires both converging and discriminating evidence. Some measures, according to the theoretical predictions, should converge—that is, show high positive or negative correlations—whereas others should discriminate—have few or no relations. This requirement led Donald T. Campbell and Donald W. Fiske to develop the convergent-discriminant, or multitrait-multimethod, technique,[48] which stems from the notion that different measures of the same variable should yield similar results, whereas different variables should yield different results regardless of the measure employed. Operationally, this implies that correlation coefficients among scores for a given variable measured by different measures should be higher than correlations among different variables measured by similar measures. Evidence of construct validity must therefore make use of both convergent and discriminant principles. The validation process requires the computation of intercorrelations among measures that represent at least two variables, each measured in at least two different ways.

Reliability

Some error is involved in any type of measurement. Reliability is an indication of the extent to which a measure contains variable errors—that is, errors that differed from one object to the next during any given measurement and that varied from time to time for a given object measured twice by the same measure. For instance, if one measures with a ruler the length of an object at two points of time and gets slightly different results, the measuring instrument contains variable errors.

Each measure consists of two components: a true component and an error component. Reliability is defined as the ratio of the true-score variance to the variance in the scores as measured. Algebraically, each person's observed score can be represented as:

$$x_i = t_i + e_i \qquad (4.5)$$

where x_i stands for the score actually obtained by person i, t_i for the true score for person i, and e_i for the amount of error that occurred for person i at the time the measurement was made. Expressed in variance terms:

$$\sigma_x^2 = \sigma_t^2 + \sigma_e^2$$

where σ_x^2 is the variance of the observed scores, σ_t^2 the variance of true scores, and σ_e^2 the variance of errors.

Reliability, defined as the ratio of true-score variance to observed-score variance, can be expressed as:

$$\text{Reliability} = \frac{\sigma_t^2}{\sigma_x^2} = \frac{\sigma_x^2 - \sigma_e^2}{\sigma_x^2} \qquad (4.6)$$

From equation 4.6 it can be seen that if the measurement involves nothing but error, then $\sigma_x^2 = \sigma_e^2$ and the reliability is zero. On the other hand, when there is no variable error at all, $\sigma_e^2 = 0$, and the ratio defined as reliability becomes:

$$\frac{\sigma_x^2}{\sigma_x^2} = 1$$

Reliability varies on a scale from zero to 1, having the former value when the measurement involves nothing but error, and reaching 1 when there is no variable error at all in the measurement. In practice, it is impossible to calculate the true score directly, independently of the amount of error that occurs in any particular measurement. Consequently, the ratio σ_t^2/σ_x^2 has to be estimated. There are three major techniques for estimating reliability: test-retest, parallel forms, and split-half.

Test-Retest   The test-retest technique corresponds most closely to the conceptual notion of reliability. A measure is administered to the same group of persons at two different times, and the correlation between the two sets of observations is computed. The obtained coefficient is the reliability estimate. With this method, error is defined as anything that leads a person to get a different score on one measurement from what he or she obtained on another measurement. Symbolically,

$$r_{xx'} = \frac{S_t{}^2}{S_x{}^2} \tag{4.7}$$

where $r_{xx'}$ stands for the correlation between performances on the first and second measurements, $S_t{}^2$ for the estimated variance of the true scores, and $S_x{}^2$ for the calculated variance of the observed scores. The correlation coefficient $r_{xx'}$ provides an estimate of reliability defined as a ratio of the true variance to the observed variance.

The test-retest technique has two limitations. First, the fact that an individual has been tested on one occasion may influence the measurement on subsequent tests. If the instrument is a questionnaire, the individual may remember specific questions and simply respond in the same way as on the first administration, thus yielding a high but overestimated reliability estimate. Second, some phenomena are continually changing. It is possible that changes may have occurred in the measured property during the measurement interval, thus lowering the estimate of reliability. The test-retest technique, then, may either overestimate or underestimate the true reliability of the instrument, and in many cases it is difficult to determine which has occurred.

Parallel Forms   One way of overcoming the limitations of the test-retest technique is through the use of parallel forms. This method requires two forms of a measuring instrument that may be considered parallel. The two forms are then administered to a group of persons (or other units of analysis), and the two sets of measures are correlated to obtain an estimate of reliability. With this technique, there is the problem of determining whether the two forms of an instrument are in fact parallel. Although statistical tests have been developed to determine whether the forms are parallel in terms of statistical measures, checking with respect to the content of the forms is done on a judgmental basis.

Split-Half   The split-half technique estimates reliability by treating each of two or more parts of a measuring instrument as a separate scale. Suppose the measuring instrument is a questionnaire. The questionnaire is separated into two sets, using the odd-numbered questions for one set and the even-numbered questions for the other. Each of the two sets of questions is treated separately and scored accordingly. The two sets are then correlated, and this is taken as an estimate of reliability. To correct the correlation coefficient obtained between the two halves, the following formula, known as the Spearman-Brown prophecy formula, may be applied:

$$r_{xx'} = \frac{2r_{oe}}{1 + r_{oe}} \tag{4.8}$$

where $r_{xx'}$ stands for the reliability of the original test, and r_{oe} for the reliability coefficient obtained by correlating the scores of the odd statements with the scores of the even statements. This correction assumes that an instrument that is $2n$ items long will be more reliable than an instrument that is n items long, and that since the length of the instrument has been halved by dividing it into odds and evens, the full instrument will have a higher reliability than would either half.

Reliability and Generalizability   Lee J. Cronbach, Nageswari Rajaratnam, and Goldine C. Gleser introduced a revision to the traditional concept of reliability.[49] These authors maintain that the chief concern of reliability theory is to answer the question "To what universe of potential measurements do we wish to generalize?" Thus, instead of reliability, the notion of generalizability is invoked. Generalizability implies that what one really wants to know about a set of measures is: To what extent and with respect to what properties are they like other sets of measures one might have taken from a given universe of potential measures? And to what extent and with respect to what properties do they differ from other measures one might have drawn from that universe of potential measures? If one asks the likeness and difference questions with respect to a universe of potential measures, one is asking about the limits of generalizability of the results of a set of measures. Whether a researcher considers a particular relation among measures to be evidence of reliability or generalizability depends on how he or she chooses to define likeness and difference of conditions and measures. The construction of what is same and what is different in sets of measures depends in turn upon the research problem.[50]

NOTES

1. Eugene J. Webb et al., *Unobtrusive Measures: Nonreactive Research in the Social Sciences* (Chicago: Rand McNally, 1966), chap. 1.
2. See also Stephen Richardson, Barbara S. Dohrenwend, and David Klein, *Interviewing: Its Forms and Functions* (New York: Basic Books, 1965); Raymond L. Gorden, *Interviewing: Strategy, Techniques and Tactics* (Homewood, Ill.: Dorsey, 1969); and Carol H. Weiss, "Interviewing in Evaluation Research," in Elmer L. Struening and Marcia Guttentag, eds., *Handbook of Evaluation Research*, I (Beverly Hills, Calif.: Sage, 1975), pp. 355–395.
3. For these and other issues in questionnaire construction, see Abraham N. Oppenheim, *Questionnaire Design and Attitude Measurement* (New York: Basic Books, 1966).
4. For other issues involved in observation, see Karl E. Weick, "Systematic Observational Methods," in Gardner Lindzey and Elliot Aronson, eds., *The Handbook of Social Psychology*, II (Reading, Mass.: Addison-Wesley, 1968), pp. 357–451.
5. Robert C. Angell, "The Moral Integration of American Cities," *American Journal of Sociology*, 57 (January 1951), 1–140.
6. Abbott S. Weinstein, "Evaluation Through Medical Records and Related Information Systems," in Struening and Guttentag, eds., *Handbook of Evaluation Research*, pp. 397–481.
7. For the problems involved in working with data banks, see Ralph L. Bisco, ed., *Data Banks, Computers and the Social Sciences* (New York: Wiley-Interscience, 1970); and Daniel Wilner et al., "Data Bank and Program Evaluation," *Evaluation*, 3, No. 3 (1973), 3–6. For a directory of social research centers in the United States and abroad, see Delbert C. Miller, *Handbook of Research Design and Social Measurement*, 3rd ed. (New York: McKay, 1977), pp. 128–139.
8. Eleanor B. Sheldon and Howard E. Freeman, "Notes on Social Indicators: Promises and Potential," *Policy Sciences*, 1 (Spring 1970), 97.
9. U.S. Department of Health, Education, and Welfare, *Toward a Social Report* (Washington, D.C.: U.S. Government Printing Office, 1969), p. xiii.
10. It is argued that social indicators can serve other purposes, including descriptive reporting and planned development. See, for example, Raymond A. Bauer, ed., *Social Indicators* (Cambridge, Mass.: M.I.T. Press, 1966); and Ralph M. Brooks, "Social Planning and Societal Monitoring," in Leslie D. Wilcox et al., eds., *Social Indicators and Societal Monitoring: An Annotated Bibliography* (San Francisco: Jossey-Bass, 1972).

11. Kenneth C. Land, "Social Indicator Models: An Overview," in Kenneth C. Land and Seymour Spilerman, eds., *Social Indicator Models* (New York: Russell Sage Foundation, 1975), pp. 5–36.

12. Eleanor B. Sheldon and Kenneth C. Land, "Social Reporting for the 1970's: A Review and Programmatic Statement," *Policy Sciences,* 3 (July 1972), 141–142.

13. *Toward a Social Report,* p. 142.

14. Sheldon and Land, "Social Reporting for the 1970's."

15. Robert Park and Eleanor B. Sheldon, "Social Indicators One Year Later: An Overview," in Robert L. Clewett and Jerry C. Olson, eds., *Social Indicators and Marketing* (Washington, D.C.: American Marketing Association, 1974), p. 13. For a basic reference document on the statistical programs of the United States government, see U.S. Bureau of the Budget, Office of Statistical Standards, *Statistical Services of the United States Government,* rev. ed. (Washington, D.C.: U.S. Government Printing Office, 1968).

16. Park and Sheldon, "Social Indicators One Year Later," p. 14. For the problems involved in developing useful measures and proposals for improvements, see *U.S. President's Commission on Federal Statistics* (Washington, D.C.: U.S. Government Printing Office, 1971).

17. Otis Dudley Duncan, *Toward Social Reporting: Next Steps,* Paper No. 2 in Social Science Frontier Series (New York: Russell Sage Foundation, 1969).

18. See Otis Dudley Duncan, "Measuring Social Change via Replication of Surveys," in Land and Spilerman, eds., *Social Indicator Models,* pp. 105–127. The following account leans on this work.

19. Ibid., p. 108.

20. Richard Stone, "Transition and Admission Models in Social Indicators," in Land and Spilerman, eds., *Social Indicator Models,* pp. 253–300.

21. James S. Coleman, "Analysis of Occupational Mobility by Models of Occupational Flow," in Land and Spilerman, eds., *Social Indicator Models,* p. 333.

22. See, for example, Angus Campbell, Philip E. Converse, and Willard L. Rodgers, *The Quality of American Life: Perceptions, Evaluations, and Satisfactions* (New York: Russell Sage Foundation, 1976).

23. See, for example, *The 1972–73 Quality of Employment Survey: Survey Descriptive Statistics with Comparison Data from the 1969–70 Survey of Working Conditions* (Ann Arbor, Mich.: Institute for Social Research, 1974).

24. See Neal Q. Herrick and Robert P. Quinn, "The Working Conditions Survey as a Source of Social Indicators," *Monthly Labor Review,* 23 (April 1971), 15–24; and Louis Guttman, "Social Problem Indicators," *Annals of the American Academy of Political and Social Science,* 393 (January 1971), 40–46.

25. S. S. Stevens, "Mathematics, Measurement and Psychophysics," in S. S. Stevens, ed., *Handbook of Experimental Psychology* (New York: Wiley, 1951), pp. 1–49.

26. Sidney Siegel, *Nonparametric Statistics for the Behavioral Sciences* (New York: McGraw-Hill, 1965), p. 22.

27. With properties that have natural zero points a ratio scale can be obtained. Since for all practical reasons ratio scales are similar to interval scales, I don't discuss their mathematical properties. The interested reader may consult Stevens, "Mathematics, Measurement and Psychophysics."

28. See, for example, Sanford Labovitz, "Some Observations on Measurement and Statistics," *Social Forces*, 46 (December 1967), 151–160; and Richard P. Boyle, "Path Analysis and Ordinal Data," *American Journal of Sociology*, 75 (January 1970), 461–480.

29. Thomas Wilson, "Critique of Ordinal Variables," in Hubert M. Blalock, Jr., ed., *Causal Models in the Social Sciences* (Chicago: Aldine, 1971), p. 428.

30. Boyle, "Path Analysis and Ordinal Data," p. 479.

31. Louis Guttman, "A Basis for Scaling Qualitative Data," *American Sociological Review*, 9 (February 1944), 139–150. See also Norman H. Nie et al., *Statistical Package for the Social Sciences*, 2nd ed. (New York: McGraw-Hill, 1975), pp. 528–535; and John A. Stookey and Michael A. Baer, "A Critique of Guttman Scaling: With Special Attention to Its Applications to the Study of Collegial Bodies," *Quality and Quantity*, 10 (October 1976), 251–260.

32. Nie et al., *Statistical Package for the Social Sciences*, p. 529.

33. For a somewhat different but in fact complementary interpretation of the characteristics of a scale, see Herbert Menzel, "A New Coefficient for Scalogram Analysis," *Public Opinion Quarterly*, 17 (Summer 1953), 268–280.

34. Bonnie Bullough, "Poverty, Ethnic Identity and Preventive Health Care," *Journal of Health and Social Behavior*, 13 (December 1972), 347–359.

35. For a more detailed description of Likert scales, see Oppenheim, *Questionnaire Design and Attitude Measurement*, pp. 133–142.

36. Roger N. Shepard, "Introduction to Volume I," in Roger N. Shepard, A. Kimball Romney, and Sara Beth Nerlove, eds., *Multidimensional Scaling* (New York: Seminar Press, 1972), p. 8. The computational techniques involved in multidimensional scaling are beyond the scope of this book; the interested reader will find Shepard, Romney, and Nerlove, eds., ibid., Vols. I and II, and Paul E. Green and Vithala R. Rao, *Applied Multidimensional Scaling* (New York: Holt, Rinehart & Winston, 1972), most useful.

37. In recent years several handbooks of measures have been published as guides for research. See, for example, Charles M. Bonjean, Richard J. Hill, and S. Dale McLemore, *Sociological Measurement: An Inventory of Scales and Indices* (San Francisco: Chandler, 1967); Miller, *Handbook of Research Design and Social Measurement;* Leo G. Reeder, Linda Ramacher, and Sally Gorelnik, *Handbook of Scales and Indices of Health Behavior* (Pacific Palisades, Calif.: Goodyear, 1976); John P. Robinson, Jerrold G. Rusk, and Kendra B. Head, *Measures of Political Attitudes* (Ann Arbor: Survey Research Center, University of Michigan, 1968); John P. Robinson and Phillip R. Shaver, *Measures of Social Psychological Attitudes* (Ann Arbor: Survey Research Center, University of Michigan, 1969); and Paul N. Cheremisinoff, ed., *Industrial Pollution Control: Measurement and Instrumentation*

(Westport, Conn.: Technomic, 1976).

38. The following description is based on U.S. Bureau of Labor Statistics, *The Consumer Price Index: A Short Description of the Index as Revised* (Washington, D.C.: U.S. Government Printing Office, 1964); and William H. Wallace, *Measuring Price Changes: A Study of Price Indexes* (Richmond, Va.: Federal Reserve Bank of Richmond, 1970).

39. The frequencies are reported in W. Boyd Littrell, "The Problem of Jurisdiction and Official Statistics of Crime," in W. Boyd Littrell and Gideon Sjoberg eds., *Current Issues of Social Policy* (Beverly Hills, Calif.: Sage, 1976), p. 236.

40. The base of an index can be shifted by other methods. See, for example, William C. Merril and Karl A. Fox, *Introduction to Economic Statistics* (New York: Wiley, 1970), pp. 57–64.

41. For other methods of aggregation, see Merril and Fox, ibid., chap. 3; and Michael T. Hannan, *Aggregation and Disaggregation in Sociology* (Lexington, Mass.: Lexington Books, 1971).

42. For this and other problems involved in crime reports, see, for example, Sophia M. Robison, "A Critical View of the Uniform Crime Reports," *University of Michigan Law Review,* 64 (April 1966), 1031–1054; and Hans Zeisel, "The Future of Law Enforcement Statistics: A Summary View," in *U.S. President's Commission on Federal Statistics,* pp. 531–555.

43. Thorsten Sellin and Marvin E. Wolfgang, *The Measurement of Delinquency* (New York: Wiley, 1964).

44. The index has been criticized on a number of points, including the choice of samples. See, for example, G. Rose, "Concerning the Measurement of Delinquency," *British Journal of Criminology,* 6 (October 1966), 414–421.

45. The idea of a correlation and methods for computing the correlation coefficient are presented in chapter five.

46. Lee J. Cronbach, *Essentials of Psychological Testing* (New York: Harper & Row, 1960), p. 104.

47. Lee J. Cronbach and Paul E. Meehl, "Construct Validity in Psychological Tests," *Psychological Bulletin,* 52 (July 1955), 281–302.

48. Donald T. Campbell and Donald W. Fiske, "Convergent and Discriminant Validation by the Multitrait-Multimethod Matrix," *Psychological Bulletin,* 56 (March 1959), 81–105.

49. Lee J. Cronbach, Nageswari Rajaratnam, and Goldine C. Gleser, "Theory of Generalizability: A Liberalization of Reliability Theory," *British Journal of Statistical Psychology,* 16 (February 1963), 137–163.

50. For the mathematical rationale and the computational procedures of the generalizability index, see Cronbach, Rajaratnam, and Gleser, "Theory of Generalizability"; and Goldine C. Gleser, Lee J. Cronbach, and Nageswari Rajaratnam, "Generalizability of Scores Influenced by Multiple Scores of Variance," *Psychometrika,* 30 (December 1965), 395–418.

Chapter Five

Regression as a Data-Analysis System

Earlier, the argument was made that regression analysis is a general data-analytic system that most readily suits policy evaluation research. Regression analysis is one of the more powerful statistical tools, and as such it provides quantitative expressions of the manner in which two or more variables relate mathematically. This chapter elaborates on these observations from conceptual and statistical points of view.

LINEAR REGRESSION

The problem of predicting or estimating the value of a target variable that corresponds to a given value of a program variable requires that a mathematical expression in equation form be derived. Such expressions convey functional relationships. The relationship in which the value of a target variable, Y, can be determined exactly from the specified values of a program variable, X, is expressed by $Y = f(X)$, which reads Y is a function of X. However, for most problems involved in policy evaluation research, the values of a target variable cannot be determined exactly from a set of specified values of program variables. Nevertheless, such relationships can be estimated.

The purpose of regression analysis is to determine what mathematical function best describes the relationship between X and Y. Since each X value has a corresponding Y value, it is possible to plot a graph that describes the bivariate distribution. Conventionally, the horizontal axis of the graph is used to represent the values of the independent (or program) variable X and the vertical axis to represent the values of the target variable Y. Each pair of corresponding X and Y values is termed a coordinate. When all the coordinates fall on a straight line, the function relating X to Y is referred to as a linear function. Symbolically:

$$Y = \alpha + \beta X$$

where α and β are parameters standing, respectively, for the Y-intercept and the slope of the line (β is also termed the *regression coefficient*). The slope of a linear function (β) indicates how many units change in Y are obtained for each unit change in X. For example, if $\beta = 3$, then Y increases three units for each unit increase in X.

Figure 5.1 illustrates the observations made so far, an example of a positive relationship. However, linear functions can also de-

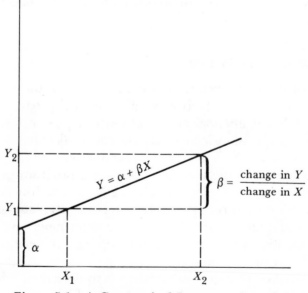

Figure 5.1 **A Geometrical Interpretation of the General Form of Linear Regression**

scribe negative relationships. For a negative relationship, the regression coefficient has a negative sign, $Y = \alpha - \beta X$, and the linear function is sloped from the upper left to the lower right on the graph. A negative regression coefficient, say $\beta = -3$, indicates that Y decreases by three units for each unit increase in X.

The parameters α and β stand for the Y-intercept and the regression coefficient in a population. In practice, however, populations are rarely being investigated. Usually random and representative samples are drawn, the findings of which are generalized to the entire population. With samples, the Y-intercept is denoted by a, the regression coefficient by b, and the linear function for a sample becomes $Y = a + bX$.

The objective of regression analysis is to formulate a function by which the researcher can predict or estimate the scores on a target variable from scores on independent variables.* With only one program variable, one starts with the observed or actual bivariate distribution and attempts to find a function that best de-

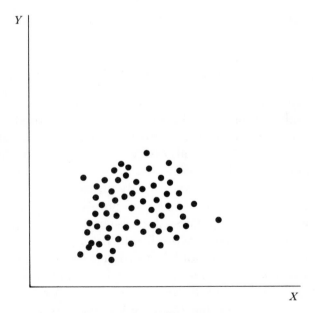

Figure 5.2   **A Scattergram**

* The terms "independent variables" and "program variables" will be used interchangeably.

scribes the relationship between the variables. In practice, the points in the graph that represent the observed coordinates almost never fall along a straight line. In such situations the graph of the coordinates is referred to as a scattergram, illustrated in Figure 5.2. With distributions such as the one shown in the figure, there is no continuous line that would connect all the points, nor is there a simple function that can relate the X and Y variables exactly. Nevertheless, a close approximation to the exact functional relationships can be formulated. One common procedure for arriving at such approximations is the least-squares method.

Linear Least-Squares

The least-squares method is a way for finding the one straight line that provides the best fit for an observed bivariate distribution. The least-squares method for the selection of a linear function that will yield the smallest sum of squared residuals can be expressed as:

$$\sum_{i=1}^{N} (Y_i - \hat{Y})^2 = \text{minimum}$$

where $\sum_{i=1}^{N} (Y_i - \hat{Y})^2$ stands for the residual sum of squares.

The meaning of the least-squares method can be seen more easily through examination of the scattergram presented in Figure 5.3. The line drawn amid the points is a linear function, although none of the points actually falls on the line. The distance between the function line and any observed point in the scattergram is termed a *residual*, and is denoted e_i. By measuring the distance of each point in the scattergram from the line (Σe_i) and finding the average of all these distances, the researcher can estimate the amount of error involved in predicting the Y scores from the X scores. Now a second line can be drawn and the average distances of the points from it can also be obtained. A comparison of these two averages would indicate the extent to which the amount of error from the first line has decreased or increased. To find the best line, that is, the line that yields the smallest average distance from all the points, more lines can be drawn until the line that minimizes the average residuals is obtained.

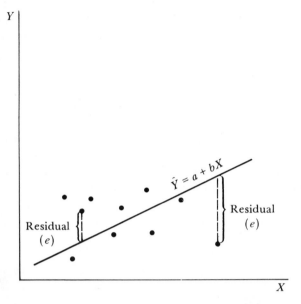

Figure 5.3   **A Geometrical Interpretation of Residuals**

Alternatively, the best-fitting line can be obtained with the following formulas that minimize the amount of error involved: [1]

$$a = \bar{Y} - b\bar{X} \qquad (5.1)$$

$$b = \frac{\sum\limits_{i=1}^{N} (X_i - \bar{X})(Y_i - \bar{Y})}{\sum\limits_{i=1}^{N} (X_i - \bar{X})^2} \qquad (5.2)$$

Equations 5.1 and 5.2 are termed the *normal equations* of bivariate regression. Since we are dealing now with a linear function that yields an estimate of Y scores from the X scores, the following expression, termed the *regression line*, will be used:

$$\hat{Y} = \hat{a} + \hat{b}X \qquad (5.3)$$

where $\hat{Y}$, $\hat{a}$, and $\hat{b}$ are estimates. Using the normal equations, the value $\Sigma (Y_i - \hat{Y}_i)^2$ is minimized. Furthermore, since the residual sum of squares is minimized, the averaged squared residuals will also be minimized:

$$S_{y \cdot x}^2 = \frac{\sum_{i=1}^{N} (Y_i - \hat{Y}_i)^2}{N - 2}$$

$$= \text{minimum for averaged squared residuals} \tag{5.4}$$

where N stands for the number of observations (number of points in the scattergram), and $N - 2$ is the degrees of freedom.[2] Equation 5.4 is termed the *residual variance*, and its square root yields the standard error of estimate (*SEE*):

$$SEE = \sqrt{\frac{\sum_{i=1}^{N} (Y_i - \hat{Y}_i)^2}{N - 2}} \tag{5.5}$$

By definition, the standard error of estimate measures the amount of error involved in predicting Y scores; a "good fit" is reflected by a relatively small standard error of estimate. When the regression line provides a perfect fit with the actual observations, the standard error of estimate is equal to zero. In fact, if one assumes that there is a true regression line, of which the least-squares line is an estimate, and in addition that the residuals are independently and normally distributed with zero means and the same standard deviation (discussed in the next section), then the normal distribution permits approximate probability statements about the errors of prediction. For example, one can state that approximately 95 percent of the errors in predictions will be less than 1.96 *SEE* in magnitude. Accordingly, it suffices to calculate the number $1.96 \times (SEE)$ and then draw two equally distanced lines parallel to the estimated regression line (above and below it) to see the approximate 95-percent prediction band,* as illustrated in Figure 5.4.

Having obtained the estimated regression line, it is also important to know whether the regression coefficient in the population

---

* Such probability statements are appropriate only for large samples.

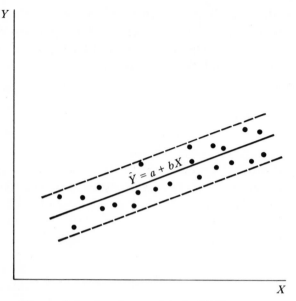

Figure 5.4   **An Approximate 95-Percent Prediction Band**

(β) differs from zero. If the regression coefficient in the population is equal to zero, then the independent variable is of no use in estimating the target variable, that is, $\hat{Y} = \bar{Y}$. A test of statistical significance and a confidence interval for the estimate of the regression coefficient has been developed from the standard error of the estimate of the regression coefficient, $\hat{b}_{SEE}$, which equals:

$$\hat{b}_{SEE} = \frac{SEE}{\sqrt{\sum (X_i - \bar{X})^2}} \tag{5.6}$$

To perform the test of statistical significance for $\beta \neq 0$, one simply considers the ratio of the estimated regression coefficient and its standard error:

$$t = \frac{\hat{b} - \beta}{\hat{b}_{SEE}} \tag{5.7}$$

where $\beta = 0$. This expression has a t distribution with $N - 2$ degrees of freedom. When the number of observations is greater than thirty, the t distribution approximates the normal distribution. This approximation implies that since for the normal distribution the two-tailed .05 limits are at ± 1.96 standard deviations, a regression coefficient should be twice its standard error if it is to be statistically significant at the .05 level of significance.[3]

Linear Correlation

The standard error of estimate is a measure of "goodness of fit" that depends on the units of measurement of the Y variable. Another measure of goodness of fit that does not depend on any units of measurement is the *coefficient of determination*. The rationale behind this measure is that the variance of the target variable Y can be divided into two parts: the explained variation and the residual variation. The variance of Y, S_y^2, is expressed:

$$S_y^2 = \frac{\sum_{i=1}^{N} (Y_i - \bar{Y})^2}{N}$$

That is, the variance is the sum of the squared deviations about the mean value of Y divided by the number of observations. This expression can be regarded as the total variation of the variable Y. On the other hand, the standard error of the estimate (equation 5.5) is the sum of the squared deviations about the regression line, and can be viewed as the residual variation of the variable Y, or the variation of Y left unexplained by the regression line, as illustrated in Figure 5.5.

For the least-squares regression line, the total variation is always larger than the residual variation because the regression line minimizes the residual variation. The explained variation of the target variable Y is the total variation less the residual variation:

$$\begin{matrix} \text{Explained} \\ \text{variation} \end{matrix} = \begin{bmatrix} \text{Total variation} \\ S_y^2 \end{bmatrix} - \begin{bmatrix} \text{Residual variation} \\ S_{\hat{e}}^2 \end{bmatrix}$$

The ratio of the variation explained by the regression line to the total variation in the target variable yields the coefficient of deter-

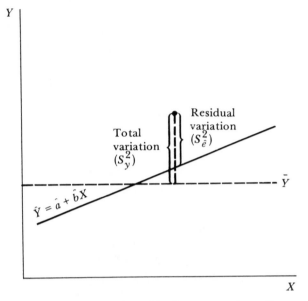

Figure 5.5   **A Graphic Interpretation of Explained and Unexplained Variation from the Regression Line**

mination, R^2:

$$R^2 = \frac{S_y^2 - S_{\hat{e}}^2}{S_y^2} \tag{5.8}$$

The coefficient of determination may vary from zero (no explained variation) to 1 for a "perfect fit" (all the variation in Y is explained by the regression line). The coefficient of determination is usually interpreted as the percentage of variation of the variable Y explained by the regression line. For computational purposes, the following formula[4] can be substituted for equation 5.8:

$$R^2 = \frac{\left[\sum_{i=1}^{N} (X_i - \bar{X})(Y_i - \bar{Y}) \right]^2}{\left[\sum_{i=1}^{N} (X_i - \bar{X})^2 \right] \left[\sum_{i=1}^{N} (Y_i - \bar{Y})^2 \right]} \tag{5.9}$$

Note that the numerator of R^2 is the same expression as in equation 5.2 for the determination of b. The expression $\Sigma (X_i - \bar{X})$ $(Y_i - \bar{Y})$ is referred to as covariation, and it measures how X and Y vary together.

In addition to the standard error of estimate and R^2, the *product-moment coefficient*, also termed Pearson's r, is often used. Pearson's r is simply the square root of the coefficient of determination:

$$r = \frac{\sum_{i=1}^{N} (X_i - \bar{X})(Y_i - \bar{Y})}{\sqrt{\left[\sum_{i=1}^{N} (X_i - \bar{X})^2\right]\left[\sum_{i=1}^{N} (Y_i - \bar{Y})^2\right]}} \tag{5.10}$$

Pearson's r differs from the coefficient of determination in that it can be positive or negative. If it is negative it indicates an inverse relationship between the variables: as the Y scores go down, the X scores tend to go up, and vice versa. This inverse relationship is also indicated by a negative slope of the estimated regression line. Pearson's r can vary from -1.0 to $+1.0$; if $r = 0$, there is no linear relationship between the variables. A significance test of r can be performed by computing the t statistics:

$$t = r \sqrt{\frac{N - 2}{1 - r^2}} \tag{5.11}$$

which has a t distribution with $N - 2$ degrees of freedom.

To exemplify the discussion so far, the first two columns in Table 5.1 report sample data for job evaluation (Y) and corresponding scores on an achievement test (X) administered at the completion of a manpower training program. The remaining columns report the computations necessary to calculate the various statistics. The calculated means for X and Y are:

$$\bar{X} = \frac{\Sigma X_i}{N} = \frac{190}{10} = 19$$

$$\bar{Y} = \frac{\Sigma Y_i}{N} = \frac{260}{10} = 26$$

Table 5.1   **Calculations for Linear Regression and Correlation Analysis**

X	Y	$(X_i-\bar{X})$	$(X_i-\bar{X})^2$	$(Y_i-\bar{Y})$	$(Y_i-\bar{Y})^2$	$(X_i-\bar{X})(Y_i-\bar{Y})$	$\hat{Y}$	$(Y_i-\hat{Y}_i)^2$
16	23	−3	9	−3	9	9	23.2	.04
20	25	1	1	−1	1	−1	26.9	3.60
27	31	8	64	5	25	40	33.5	6.25
13	18	−6	36	−8	64	48	20.3	5.30
15	22	−4	16	−4	16	16	22.2	.04
24	33	5	25	7	49	35	30.7	5.30
30	37	11	121	11	121	121	36.4	.36
11	19	−8	64	−7	49	56	18.5	.25
16	25	−3	9	−1	1	3	23.2	3.24
18	27	−1	1	1	1	−1	25.1	4.00
190	260	0	346	0	336	326	260.0	28.34

The regression coefficient is:

$$b = \frac{\sum (X_i - \bar{X})(Y_i - \bar{Y})}{\sum (X_i - \bar{X})^2} = \frac{326}{346} = .942$$

The value of the intercept is:

$$a = \bar{Y} - b\bar{X} = 26 - (.942)(19) = 8.1$$

The estimated regression equation is:

$$\hat{Y} = 8.1 + .942X$$

The regression line is drawn in Figure 5.6. The standard error of estimate is:

$$SEE = \sqrt{\frac{\sum (Y_i - \hat{Y}_i)^2}{N - 2}} = \sqrt{\frac{28.34}{8}} = 1.88$$

Even though the sample given by Table 5.1 is too small to justify a prediction band, a band will nevertheless be made for illustration. For 95 percent the prediction band is 1.96(1.88) = 3.7. From

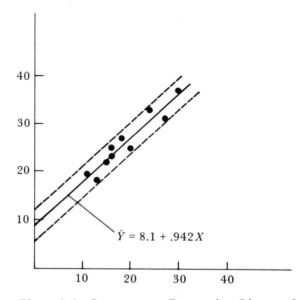

Figure 5.6 **Scattergram, Regression Line, and an Approximate 95-Percent Prediction Band**

Figure 5.6 it can be seen that all ten points lie within the 95-percent band. Thus, in the long run of similar studies one would expect approximately 95 percent of such points to lie inside the band, provided the normal distribution assumption is satisfied.

To test for the statistical significance of the regression coefficient, equation 5.7 is used:

$$t = \frac{b - 0}{\hat{b}_{SEE}} = \frac{.942}{\left(\dfrac{1.88}{\sqrt{346}}\right)} = \frac{.942}{.101} = 9.33$$

Comparing this value with the value of t in the t distribution (Appendix B) for a two-tailed test and 8 degrees of freedom, it can be observed that at a .001 level of significance the value of t is 5.041. Since the calculated value of t (9.33) is greater than 5.041, it can be concluded that the regression coefficient is significant at the .001 level; that is, the chances of $\beta = 0$ are less than .01 percent.*

* When the sample size is greater than thirty, the normal distribution (Appendix A) is used.

To calculate the coefficient of determination, equation 5.9 is used:

$$R^2 = \frac{\left[\sum_{i=1}^{N} (X_i - \bar{X})(Y_i - \bar{Y})\right]^2}{\left[\sum_{i=1}^{N} (X_i - \bar{X})^2\right]\left[\sum_{i=1}^{N} (Y_i - \bar{Y})^2\right]} = \frac{106{,}276}{(346)(336)} = .91$$

This implies that 91 percent of the statistical variance in job evaluation (Y) is explained by the achievement test (X). To find the value of Pearson's r, we can take the square root of r^2 or, alternatively, use equation 5.10:

$$r = \frac{\sum_{i=1}^{N} (X_i - \bar{X})(Y_i - \bar{Y})}{\sqrt{\left[\sum_{i=1}^{N} (X_i - \bar{X})^2\right]\left[\sum_{i=1}^{N} (Y_i - \bar{Y})^2\right]}} = \frac{326}{\sqrt{(346)(336)}} = .96$$

To test for the statistical significance of r, that is, to see whether the product-moment coefficient in the population (denoted ρ) equals zero ($\rho = 0$), equation 5.11 is used:

$$t = r\sqrt{\frac{N-2}{1-r^2}} = .95, \qquad \sqrt{\frac{8}{.09}} = 8.96$$

Comparing this value with the value of t in the t distribution for a two-tailed test at a .001 level of significance results in rejecting the possibility of $\rho = 0$ at less than a .01 percent chance of being wrong. If the sample were random and representative, one could conclude that the obtained findings hold for the entire population.

Residual Terms in Regression

Earlier, a residual, e_i, was expressed as $e_i = Y_i - \hat{Y}_i$. That is, the residual is the difference between the observed or actual Y_i and the $\hat{Y}_i$ estimate obtained from the regression calculations. Hence:

$$Y = a + bX + e_i$$

The least-squares method minimizes $\sum\limits_{i=1}^{N} (e_i)^2$ or $\sum\limits_{i=1}^{N} (Y_i - \hat{Y})^2$. Since the derivation of a and b in the regression equation is based on the residual or error term and its minimization, it is important to consider the assumptions made about the distribution of error terms.

> *Assumption I:* The distribution of error terms around the regression line is normal. The error term is viewed as an accumulation of smaller errors that produces a deviation from the regression line; these smaller errors are random (uncorrelated with one another) and additive so that they produce the normal distribution.

> *Assumption II:* The mean of the distribution of each of the distributions is equal to zero. In other words, the mean of each of the error distributions falls on the true regression line. Indeed, the least-squares method is an attempt to locate a line on the mean of the error distribution.

> *Assumption III:* Error terms are not correlated with the independent variable. This assumption implies that the various factors that cause the error terms do not vary with the values of the independent variable. If this assumption is violated, the substantive implication would be that a number of unknowns in the error term are correlated with the independent variable and thus might explain its variation.

> *Assumption IV:* There is no autocorrelation of error terms; that is, no error term should correlate with successive or preceding error terms.

These assumptions and some techniques for detecting their violations are discussed in greater detail in the following sections.

CURVILINEAR REGRESSION

The discussion has so far been confined to the linear regression model. However, relationships among variables might be nonlinear. The greater the degree to which a relationship differs from linearity, the more inappropriate the linear regression and the product-moment coefficient for representing the relationship. In some cases a nonlinear relationship can be transformed through logarithms or reciprocals to fit the linear regression model.[5] In other cases nonlinear regression models should be used.

A mathematical expression that has the form of a linear regression equation is referred to as a first-order polynomial equation. The term "first order" refers to a linear expression such as $Y = a + bX$, where X is the first degree, or order. A curvilinear expression may take the form of a higher-order polynomial such as $Y = a + bX + cX^2$, where X^2 is the second degree, or order. The general form of a polynomial expression of the estimated nonlinear regression is expressed as:

$$\hat{Y} = a + bX + cX^2 + \ldots + zX^k + e_i \qquad (5.12)$$

where k indicates the order, or degree, of the polynomial.

Consider the data reported in the first two columns of Table 5.2 and the scattergram in Figure 5.7. Obviously the relationship does not display a linear trend; a parabola is a more appropriate expression of the relationship between the variables than is a straight line. The simplest parabola is a second-order polynomial regression equation:

$$Y = a + b_1X + b_2X^2 + e_i \qquad (5.13)$$

Table 5.2   **Calculations for Curvilinear Regression**

X	Y	X^2	X^3	X^4	XY	X^2Y
3	6	9	27	81	18	54
4	7	16	64	256	28	112
4	8	16	64	256	32	128
6	9	36	216	1,296	54	324
6	11	36	216	1,296	66	396
10	12	100	1,000	10,000	120	1,200
12	13	144	1,728	20,736	156	1,872
12	12	144	1,728	20,736	144	1,728
15	12	225	3,375	50,625	180	2,700
18	10	324	5,832	104,976	180	3,240
19	9	361	6,859	130,321	171	3,249
20	7	400	8,000	160,000	140	2,800
20	9	400	8,000	160,000	180	3,600
21	6	441	9,261	194,481	126	2,646
170	131	2,652	46,370	855,060	1,595	24,049

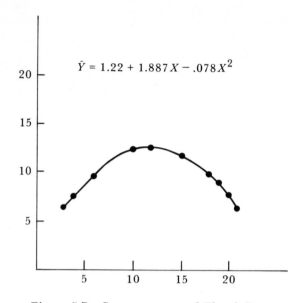

Figure 5.7   Scattergram and Fitted Curve

The least-squares equations for a second-order polynomial are:[6]

I. $$b_1 \sum X + b_2 \sum X^2 + aN = \sum Y$$

II. $$b_1 \sum X^2 + b_2 \sum X^3 + a \sum X = \sum XY \qquad (5.14)$$

III. $$b_1 \sum X^3 + b_2 \sum X^4 + a \sum X^2 = \sum X^2 Y$$

This system of equations can be extended to polynomial curves of higher degrees. For example, for a third-order polynomial:

I. $$b_1 \sum X + b_2 \sum X^2 + b_3 \sum X^3 + aN = \sum Y$$

II. $$b_1 \sum X^2 + b_2 \sum X^3 + b_3 \sum X^4 + a \sum X = \sum XY$$

III. $$b_1 \sum X^3 + b_2 \sum X^4 + b_3 \sum X^5 + a \sum X^2 = \sum X^2 Y$$

IV. $$b_1 \sum X^4 + b_2 \sum X^5 + b_3 \sum X^6 + a \sum X^3 = \sum X^2 Y$$

The four equations can be solved simultaneously to obtain the third-order polynomial regression coefficients. Generally, the *k*th-order polynomial expression involves $k + 1$ coefficients, and $k + 1$ equations are required to solve for these coefficients.

Table 5.2 shows the calculations made to solve for the coefficients in a second-order polynomial regression. The obtained totals are inserted into equation 5.14:

I. $\quad\quad\quad\quad\quad\quad b_1 170 + b_2 2{,}652 + a14 = 131$

II. $\quad\quad\quad\quad b_1 2{,}652 + b_2 46{,}370 + a170 = 1{,}595$

III. $\quad\quad b_1 46{,}370 + b_2 855{,}060 + a2{,}652 = 24{,}049$

Dividing Equation I by 14, Equation II by 170, and Equation III by 2,652 results in:

I. $\quad\quad\quad\quad b_1 12.143 + b_2 189.429 + a = 9.357$

II. $\quad\quad\quad\quad b_1 15.6 + b_2 272.765 + a = 9.382$

III. $\quad\quad\quad\quad b_1 17.485 + b_2 322.421 + a = 9.067$

or

I. $\quad\quad\quad\quad\quad\quad b_1 3.457 + b_2 83.336 = .025$

II. $\quad\quad\quad\quad\quad\quad b_1 5.342 + b_2 132.992 = -.29$

or

I. $\quad\quad\quad\quad\quad\quad b_1 + b_2 24.107 = .0072$

II. $\quad\quad\quad\quad\quad\quad b_1 + b_2 24.789 = -.0543$

Subtracting Equation I from Equation II yields the value of b_2; for our example, $b_2 = -.078$. Substituting the value of b_2 in Equation I gives $b_1 = 1.887$. Once the values of b_1 and b_2 are known, the value of a is determined by solving Equation III. In our case, $a = 1.22$. Hence:

$$\hat{Y} = 1.22 + 1.887X - .078X^2$$

The graph in Figure 5.7 shows this parabola. The standard error of estimate for a second-order polynomial regression is defined in the same way as for the linear regression except for the denominator; $N - S$ rather than $N - 2$, where S denotes the number of unknowns in equation 5.14; that is:

$$SEE = \sqrt{\frac{\sum (Y_i - \hat{Y}_i)^2}{N - S}} \tag{5.15}$$

For the previous example,

Y	6	7	8	9	11	12	13	12	12	10	9	7	9	6
$\hat{Y}$	6.18	7.52	7.52	9.7	9.7	12.29	12.6	12.6	11.9	9.9	8.9	7.8	7.8	6.4
$Y_i - \hat{Y}_i$	−.18	−.52	.48	−.7	1.3	−.29	.4	−.6	.1	.1	.1	−.8	1.2	−.4

$$SEE = \sqrt{\frac{5.59}{11}} = .713$$

When the relationships among the variables are curvilinear, Pearson's r underestimates the strength of relationships. With curvilinear relationships the correlation ratio (the Greek letter eta, η), also termed the *coefficient of curvilinear correlation,* should be used. When the relationship is linear, $r = \eta$; in curvilinear relationships, the extent to which Pearson's r is less than η is a measure of the degree to which a curvilinear relationship exists.

Eta square (η^2) can be defined as the "explained variance" divided by the "total variance," or:

$$\eta^2 = \frac{\text{explained variance}}{\text{total variance}}$$

and

$$\eta = \sqrt{\frac{\text{explained variance}}{\text{total variance}}}$$

In this sense, η^2 may be interpreted as the proportion of explained variation of Y given the values of X; this interpretation is similar to the one conveyed for r^2. Unlike Pearson's r, however, η can range from zero to $+1.00$—but it can never be negative.

MULTIPLE REGRESSION

Thus far our concern has been with estimating the values of a target variable from the values of a single independent variable. Most often, however, impact models consist of two or more program variables the values of which are used to predict the target variable. The purpose of multiple regression analysis is to estimate such multivariate models.

In multiple regression analysis, the regression equation is defined as the path of the mean of the target variable Y for all the combinations of the independent variables $X_1, X_2, X_3, \ldots, X_k$. The regression equation takes the form:

$$Y = a + b_1X_1 + b_2X_2 + b_3X_3 + \ldots + b_kX_k$$

where a stands for the intercept of the plane of regression in a k-dimensional space with the Y axis; and $b_1, b_2, b_3, \ldots, b_k$ represent the regression coefficients. The model behind this equation is that there are k multiple, independent causes of Y, the target variable, as shown in Figure 5.8. The regression coefficients in multiple

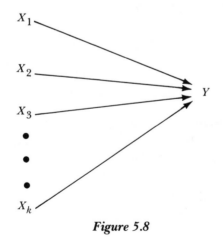

Figure 5.8

regression are interpreted as partial slopes. They indicate how much change is expected in Y when X_k, the kth independent variable, changes by one unit and all the other independent variables are statistically held constant. Thus, if the independent variables are not at all intercorrelated, the regression coefficients would be the same as if the independent variables were regressed one at a time on the target variable.

Just as in bivariate regression, the observed data can be used to estimate the intercept and the regression coefficients by the least-squares method:

$$\sum (Y_i - \hat{Y}_i)^2 = \text{minimum}$$

The result will be a unique best-fitting plane determined by the specific values of $a, b_1, b_2, b_3, \ldots, b_k$. In fact, if all the regression coefficients except one are zero, the problem reduces to the bivariate case. Thus, the estimated coefficients generate the predicted regression equation.

For two independent variables the predicted equation can be written as:

$$\hat{Y} = a + b_1 X_1 + b_2 X_2 \tag{5.16}$$

In this equation there are three unknowns $(a, b_1, \text{ and } b_2)$ and thus three equations that must be solved simultaneously:

$$\sum X_1 Y = b_1 \sum X_1^2 + b_2 \sum X_1 X_2 + a \sum X_1$$
$$\sum X_2 Y = b_1 \sum X_1 X_2 + b_2 \sum X_2^2 + a \sum X_2 \tag{5.17}$$
$$\sum Y = b_1 \sum X_1 + b_2 \sum X_2 + Na$$

This system of equations is usually referred to as normal equations.

For the reader who is unprepared to solve equations simultaneously, the following formulas for b_1, b_2, and a can be used:

$$b_1 = \frac{(\sum x_1 y)(\sum x_2^2) - (\sum x_1 x_2)(\sum x_2 y)}{(\sum x_1^2)(\sum x_2^2) - (\sum x_1 x_2)^2}$$

$$b_2 = \frac{(\sum x_1^2)(\sum x_2 y) - (\sum x_1 x_2)(\sum x_1 y)}{(\sum x_1^2)(\sum x_2^2) - (\sum x_1 x_2)^2}$$

$$a = \frac{\sum Y - b_1 \sum X_1 - b_2 \sum X_2}{N}$$

where

$$\sum x_1^2 = \sum X_1^2 - \frac{(\sum X_1)^2}{N}$$

$$\sum x_2^2 = \sum X_2^2 - \frac{(\sum X_2)^2}{N}$$

$$\sum x_1 x_2 = \sum X_1 X_2 - \frac{(\sum X_1)(\sum X_2)}{N}$$

$$\sum x_1 y = \sum X_1 Y - \frac{(\sum X_1)(\sum Y)}{N}$$

$$\sum x_2 y = \sum X_2 Y - \frac{(\sum X_2)(\sum Y)}{N}$$

To exemplify the calculations for the least-squares solution, consider the data in Table 5.3, where Y stands for the target variable and X_1 and X_2 for the independent variables:

$$b_1 = \frac{(43.8)(63.6) - (67.4)(41.2)}{(81.6)(63.6) - 4542.8} = .014$$

$$b_2 = \frac{(81.6)(41.2) - (67.4)(43.8)}{(81.6)(63.6) - 4542.8} = .633$$

$$a = \frac{51 - (.33)(52) - (.26)(48)}{10} = 1.989$$

Table 5.3 **Calculations for the Least-Squares Solution**

Y	X_1	X_2	Y^2	X_1^2	X_2^2	$X_1 Y$	$X_2 Y$	$X_1 X_2$
2	1	1	4	1	1	2	2	1
3	2	3	9	4	9	6	9	6
4	4	2	16	16	4	16	8	8
5	3	4	25	9	16	15	20	12
5	4	3	25	16	9	20	15	12
7	5	6	49	25	36	35	42	30
4	6	5	16	36	25	24	20	30
6	8	7	36	64	49	48	42	56
7	9	8	49	81	64	63	56	72
8	10	9	64	100	81	80	72	90
51	52	48	293	352	294	309	286	317

The multiple regression equation is:

$$\hat{Y} = 1.989 + .014X_1 + .633X_2$$

The general form of the trivariate regression equation is:

$$\hat{Y} = a + b_1X_1 + b_2X_2 + b_3X_3$$

To determine the least-squares solution, the following four normal equations are used:

$$\sum X_1Y = b_1 \sum X_1^2 + b_2 \sum X_1X_2 + b_3 \sum X_1X_3 + a \sum X_1$$

$$\sum X_2Y = b_1 \sum X_1X_2 + b_2 \sum X_2^2 + b_3 \sum X_2X_3 + a \sum X_2$$

$$\sum X_3Y = b_1 \sum X_1X_3 + b_2 \sum X_2X_3 + b_3 \sum X_3^2 + a \sum X_3$$

$$\sum Y = b_1 \sum X_1 + b_2 \sum X_2 + b_3 \sum X_3 + Na$$

This pattern can easily be extended to k independent variables. However, the calculations become increasingly laborious and call for the use of a computer.[7]

Once the values of $a, b_1, b_2, \ldots, b_k$ are estimated, the various measures of goodness of fit can be calculated as in the two-variable case. The standard error of estimate is:

$$SEE = \sqrt{\frac{\sum_{i=1}^{N} (Y_i - \hat{Y}_i)^2}{N - 2}} \tag{5.18}$$

For the previous example, $SEE = .941$. The coefficient of determination, R^2, is:

$$R^2 = \frac{S_y^2 - SEE}{S_y^2} \tag{5.19}$$

where

$$S_y^2 = \frac{\sum_{i=1}^{N} (Y_i - \bar{Y})^2}{N}$$

As in the two-variable case, the coefficient of determination measures the variation in the target variable Y, explained by variations in $X_1, X_2, \ldots, X_k$ as a percentage of the total variation in Y. The square root of the coefficient of determination yields the coefficient of multiple correlation, R. For the previous example, $R^2 = .81$ (that is, the independent variables explain 81 percent of the variance), and $R = .90$.

Performance Indicators in Education   One ambitious application of multivariate regression is the project known as Performance Indicators in Education. Essentially, this is an attempt to develop an evaluation model that relates input and environmental variables to performance outputs of local school districts.[8] Instead of assessing directly the effectiveness of specific educational programs, the researchers have centered on the large number of non-instructional variables (including community and student characteristics) presumed to have a greater predictive utility than typical instructional variables. The model has been used to calculate the expected performance for a school district, given its characteristics. To the extent that a given program exceeds or falls short of the expected performance level, the program is judged to be effective or ineffective.

One version of the model took the following as inputs, environmental characteristics, and performance:

Input

X_1 Mean of 1967 and 1968 district means in first grade reading tests

X_2 Mean of 1967 and 1968 district standard deviations in first grade reading tests

Environmental characteristics

X_3 Full tax valuation of district, divided by enrollment

X_4 Proportion of minority group students in third grade in 1970

X_5 Enrollment in grades 1–12, divided by 1,000

X_6 Square miles in district divided by number of students (i.e., density)

Performance

Y Third grade reading mean for 1970

By examining historical data on the schools in New York State, the researchers performed multivariate regression analyses of the form $\hat{Y} = a + b_1X_1 + b_2X_2 + b_3X_3 + \ldots + b_nX_n$. Using the actual data, the following result was obtained:

$$\hat{Y} = 14.75 + .298X_1 - .112X_2 + .030X_3$$
$$- 5.221X_4 + .13X_5 - 1.614X_6$$

This equation accounts for 33 percent of the variance in reading performance in the third grade. Now, for any specific set of values for a given school district, one can calculate the expected value for reading performance in the district.

Multicollinearity

If two or more independent variables are highly intercorrelated ($r > .85$), it becomes difficult to distinguish the separate effects of these variables on the target variable. Even though it may be quite obvious that the combined effect of, say, X_1 and X_2, on the target variable Y is significant, a high correlation between them makes distinguishing their separate effects problematic. This problem, termed *multicollinearity*, poses difficulties in analyzing pre-experimental and quasi-experimental data when no comparison group is available. The problem can be remedied to a certain extent by combining highly correlated independent variables into a single variable (for example, an index) or by eliminating all but one of the highly correlated independent variables.[9]

TIME-SERIES ANALYSIS

One frequent use of regression analysis is with time series. The regression coefficient can be used as a measure of trend over time. That is, "time" can be used as a variable with values from zero (the first observation) to n (the observation in the last time period) and can be regressed as an independent variable on other target variables. To the extent that the regression coefficient of time approaches zero, there is no linear trend in the target variable over time. For policy evaluation research, time series present one of the more powerful quasi-experimental designs (see chapter three). This section focuses on some data-analysis aspects of time series.

Components of Time Series

Time series are conventionally decomposed into four components: the long-term trend, seasonal variations, cyclical variations, and erratic variations.

Long-term trends in time series are the long-term movements of the series that can be characterized by steady or only slightly variable rates of change. When the data have a steady rate of change, such trends can be represented by straight lines; when the rate of change is slightly variable, the trends can be represented by smooth curves. For example, the time series illustrated in Figure 5.9 has a downward trend that can be represented with a smooth curve.

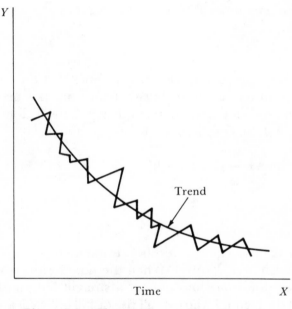

Figure 5.9 **Observations with a Curved
Downward Trend**

Seasonal variations in a time series, as the term suggests, are those variations that occur periodically at a particular time each year; fuel-oil consumption, employment rates, wage rates are affected by seasonal variations.

Cyclical variations are movements in a time series that are recurrent but unlike seasonal variations occur in cycles of length other than one year. Such variations can be found in time series recorded on an annual basis as well as in data recorded at more frequent intervals. Cyclical variations are generally longer than seasonal variations; they tend to be irregular in their elapsed time, amplitude, and occurrence. For example, hospital census varies by day of the week; auto accidents vary by the day of the week as well as by time of day.

Erratic variations are the movements left in a time series when long-term trends, seasonal variations, and cyclical variations have been identified; they are often caused by factors such as critical elections, major policy shifts, and wars.

If the letters T, S, C, and E are used to represent the four components of long-term trend, seasonal, cyclical, and erratic variations, the time series Y may be expressed as:

$$Y = T \times S \times C \times E \qquad (5.20)$$

This is a multiplicative model that assumes that the four components have different causes but that they are not necessarily independent and can affect one another.[10] Thus if, for instance, $T = 400$, $S = 1.40$, $C = 1.20$, and $E = .35$, then:

$$Y = (400)(1.40)(1.20)(.35) = 235.2$$

Linear Long-Term Trends

When the data in a time series show evidence of a long-term trend, the trend can be measured. When the time series shows a steady upward or downward movement, a straight line can be used to represent the trend. If the overall rise or fall occurs at an increasing or decreasing rate, a curved line should be used. In either case, however, the least-squares method can be used for finding a trend line. Furthermore, even for data for which the overall trend is curvilinear, linearity may be assumed for various segments and straight lines fitted to them. This is the case when the series movements tend to be slow; a straight line can adequately describe slow movements within a short time span.

The procedure for fitting a straight line to long-term trend data is the same as for fitting a regression least-squares line to pairs of points on a scattergram. The general equation of a straight line may be expressed as:

$$\hat{Y}_t = a + bX \tag{5.21}$$

where $\hat{Y}_t$ stands for the estimated trend value of the given variable at time t; a represents the Y-intercept or the estimated trend value of Y when $X = 0$; b stands for the amount of change in the trend of Y as time changes by 1 unit; and X denotes the number of time units measured from a specified origin. To determine the values of the slope and the intercept in a manner that minimizes the average residuals, equations 5.2 and 5.1 can be used. Since in time-series analysis the values of X are coded values representing time, it is possible to set them up so that:

$$\sum_{i=1}^{N} X_i = 0$$

When this is done, one term in each of the two equations is equal to zero. The coding of X is done in the following manner:

If n is odd, then:

Year	X
1	−2
2	−1
3	0
4	1
5	2
TOTAL	0

X unit is one year

If n is even, then:

Year	X
1	−3
2	−1
3	1
4	3
TOTAL	0

X unit is one-half year

To exemplify these calculations, consider the data in Table 5.4, where the number of satellites (Y) launched by the United States

Table 5.4 **Computations for Finding the Values of a Trend**

Year	Y	X	XY	X^2	Trend of Y $(\hat{Y}_t)$
1965	24	−4	−96	16	29.42
1966	33	−3	−99	9	34.49
1967	41	−2	−82	4	39.56
1968	48	−1	−48	1	44.63
1969	54	0	0	0	49.70
1970	58	1	58	1	54.77
1971	61	2	122	4	59.84
1972	63	3	189	9	64.91
1973	65	4	260	16	69.98
TOTAL	447	0	304	60	447.30

is reported by year.[11] According to these data:

$$b = \frac{\sum XY}{\sum X^2} = \frac{304}{60} = 5.07$$

$$a = \frac{\sum Y}{N} = \frac{447}{9} = 49.7$$

The least-squares regression trend is:

$$\hat{Y}_t = 49.7 + 5.07X \text{ (origin: 1969, } X = 1 \text{ year)}$$

The last column to the right in Table 5.4 reports $\hat{Y}_t$, the predicted values of Y. These were calculated by inserting the various X scores for the respective years into the trend equation.

Once the equation has been defined, the origin can be shifted from one date to another. To move the origin to a more recent date, the X in the equation is replaced by X plus the number of X units between the old and the new origins. For example, if we wished to move the origin to 1971 in the "satellites equation," the change would involve three X units, and the new trend equation would be:

$$\hat{Y}_t = 49.7 + 5.07(X + 3)$$

The time units of trend equations can be changed from years to months or from months to quarters by using the following rule: Multiply X in the original equation by a factor which represents the ratio of the size of the new X unit to the size of the old unit. For example, to change the X unit from years to quarters, the factor is one to four, or 1/4. The new equation is:

$$\hat{Y}_t = 49.7 + 5.07 \left(\frac{X}{4}\right)$$

and

$$\hat{Y}_t = 49.7 + 1.3X$$

Short-Term Analysis

So far, our concern has been with measuring linear long-term trends. This section considers time-series components whose effects cover a shorter period. These are termed short-term components of time series, or seasonal, cyclical, and erratic components.

There are various methods for measuring short-term variations; most involve computing seasonal indices. *Seasonal indices* are numbers that vary from a base of 100 (see chapter four). For example, when a seasonal period (a week, a month, or a quarter) is assigned an index value of 100, this implies that the period has no seasonal variation. The more common method of calculating seasonal indices involves comparing each season's actual value with a yearly moving average. The obtained indices are then averaged over all the time periods in the series.[12] Table 5.5 presents five years of quarterly data for a hypothetical target variable. In this example, seasonal indices are calculated by comparing actual scores with a four-quarter moving average. The first four steps in calculating the seasonal index are shown in Table 5.5 and the next two steps in Table 5.6.

In the first step, a four-quarter moving total has to be determined (column II, Table 5.5). A moving average can be computed by dividing this total by 4. Obviously a question arises of which quarter this moving average should be assigned to. When the number of periods is odd, each of the moving-average values can be assigned to the middle period; for example, with a five-point period it will be the third period. When the number of periods is

Table 5.5 Calculations for Steps One to Four in Computing Seasonal Indices

Year	Quarter	I Actual Data	II Four-quarter Moving Total of Col. I	III Two-quarter Moving Total of Col. II	IV Four-quarter Moving Average	V Actual Data as % of Moving Average
1973	First	26	—	—	—	—
	Second	29	—	—	—	—
			113			
	Third	27		229	28.6	94.4
			116			
	Fourth	31		240	30.0	103.3
			124			
1974	First	29		255	31.9	90.9
			131			
	Second	37		272	34.0	108.8
			141			
	Third	34		285	35.6	95.5
			144			
	Fourth	41		300	37.5	109.3
			156			
1975	First	32		311	38.9	82.2
			155			
	Second	49		307	38.4	127.6
			152			
	Third	33		302	37.8	87.3
			150			
	Fourth	38		287	35.9	105.8
			137			
1976	First	30		275	34.4	87.2
			138			
	Second	36		277	34.6	104.0
			139			
	Third	34		281	35.1	96.9
			142			
	Fourth	39		291	36.4	107.1
			149			
1977	First	33		305	38.1	86.6
			156			
	Second	43		317	39.6	108.6
			161			
	Third	41		—	—	—
	Fourth	44	—	—	—	—

Table 5.6 **Calculations for Steps Five and Six in Computing Seasonal Indices**

Year	Quarter			
	FIRST	SECOND	THIRD	FOURTH
1973	—	—	94.4	103.3
1974	90.9	108.8	95.5	109.3
1975	82.2	127.6	87.3	105.8
1976	87.2	104.0	96.9	107.1
1977	86.6	108.6	—	—
Mean percentage	86.7	112.3	93.5	106.4
Total of percentages				398.9
Seasonal index	86.9	112.6	93.8	106.7
Total of seasonal indices				400.0

even (four-point periods in Table 5.5), the "middle" of the four quarters is between the second and third quarters; thus the moving totals in column II are centered between the quarters.

The next two steps involve calculating a moving average that can be assigned to a particular quarter, for which two operations must be executed: (1) formulating a two-quarter moving total from the four-quarter moving-total column (column III, Table 5.5), and (2) obtaining a four-quarter moving average, which is done by dividing column III by 8, since the moving totals in this column are sums of eight quarterly values. This four-quarter moving average is centered on a particular quarter.

In the fourth step, the actual score for each quarter is expressed as a percentage of its moving average (column V). In the fifth step (shown in Table 5.6), the mean percentage value from step 4 over all the years is computed. For example, the mean percentage value for the first quarter is [90.9 + 82.2 + 87.2 + 86.6]/4 = 86.7. This value implies that on the average the score for the first quarter was 86.7 percent of the four-quarter moving average centered on the first quarter. The last step (also shown in Table 5.6) consists of adjusting the mean percentages so that they add up to a total of 400. This is done by multiplying each mean percentage value by an adjustment factor of 400/398.9, or 1.003. The result is a new percentage value which varies from a base of 100 and represents the seasonal index.

The procedure outlined for this example is similar to that which would be followed in computing monthly seasonal indices: (1) calculation of a twelve-month moving total, (2) formation of a two-month moving total from the twelve-month moving total, (3) computation of a twelve-month moving average, (4) conversion of each month's actual figures into a percentage of its moving average, (5) listing for each month the mean percentage value from step 4 over all years, and (6) adjustment of the mean percentages so that they add up to a total of 1,200.

Measuring Variations by Decomposition

Given a multiplication model of the form $Y = T \times S \times C \times E$, and given that the values for T and S are known, the components $C \times E$ can be determined by decomposition as:

$$\frac{Y}{T \times S} = \frac{T \times S \times C \times E}{T \times S} = C \times E \tag{5.22}$$

After this initial decomposition, the $C \times E$ observations can be used to calculate E by methods such as the moving average to find the value of C. Alternatively, $C \times E$ can be considered to represent one component (CE) and the form of the general equation can be expressed as:

$$Y = T \times S \times CE \tag{5.23}$$

Autocorrelation

Time-series data consist of observations of a variable at different points of time. Consequently, there is usually a mutual dependence of successive observations. This lack of independence may seriously affect the interpretation of the least-squares estimates. In other words, an observed value of Y in a time series may be correlated with, but not independent of, the value of the same variable in the previous time period. This type of correlation is termed the *coefficient of autocorrelation* and is denoted ρ. One way to determine the presence of autocorrelation is to examine the pattern of residuals or errors from a regression line. For example, the residuals in Figure 5.10 indicate that the error term is autocorrelated.[13]

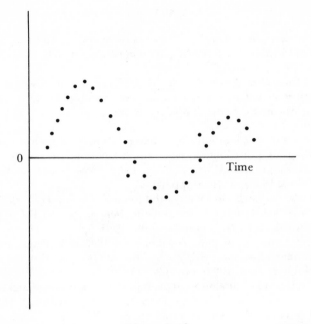

Figure 5.10

The coefficient of autocorrelation can be estimated with the formula:

$$\rho = \frac{\sum\limits_{i=1}^{N} \hat{e}\hat{e}_{i-1}}{\sum\limits_{i=1}^{N} \hat{e}_{i}^{2}} \tag{5.24}$$

where $\hat{e}_i$ is the estimated error term. The obtained ρ value is used to transform the variables and compute a new regression equation. The general form for the modified equation is:

$$\hat{Y} = a(1 - \rho) + bX \tag{5.25}$$

For instance, if the original estimated equation is $\hat{Y}_t = 49.7 + 5.07X$, and if $\rho = .570$, then the modified equation is $\hat{Y}_t = 49.7 (1 - .570) + 5.07X$, or $\hat{Y}_t = 21.4 + 5.07X$.

NOTES

1. For the derivation of the least-squares estimates, see Gouri K. Bhattacharyya and Richard A. Johnson, *Statistical Concepts and Methods* (New York: Wiley, 1977), p. 346.
2. The term *degrees of freedom* is discussed in any statistics textbook. It is used to ensure an unbiased estimate. See, for example, David Nachmias and Chava Nachmias, *Research Methods in the Social Sciences* (New York: St. Martin's, 1976), pp. 282–283.
3. Readers unfamiliar with the logic and procedures of statistical inferences, including the *t* distribution, may consult any standard statistics textbook.
4. See Charles R. Frank, Jr., *Statistics and Econometrics* (New York: Holt, Rinehart & Winston, 1971), pp. 56–57.
5. See, for example, Bhattacharyya and Johnson, *Statistical Concepts and Methods*, pp. 379–384; and Edward R. Tufte, *Data Analysis for Politics and Policy* (Englewood Cliffs, N.J.: Prentice-Hall, 1974), pp. 108–131.
6. For the derivation of these equations, see William S. Peters and George W. Summers, *Statistical Analysis for Business Decisions* (Englewood Cliffs, N.J.: Prentice-Hall, 1968), pp. 362–373.
7. One useful and commonly used package of computer programs is Norman H. Nie et al., *Statistical Package for the Social Sciences*, 2nd ed. (New York: McGraw-Hill, 1975); see especially pp. 276–372.
8. Edmund H. Weiss, "Models in Educational Planning and Operations," in Saul I. Gass and Roger L. Sisson, eds., *A Guide to Models in Governmental Planning and Operations* (Potomac, Md.: Sauger, 1975), pp. 279–316.
9. See Frank, *Statistics and Econometrics*, pp. 295–297; and Donald E. Farrar and Robert R. Glauber, "Multicollinearity in Regression Analysis: The Problem Revisited," *Review of Economics and Statistics*, 49 (February 1967), pp. 92–107.
10. Occasionally an additive model in which $Y = T + S + C + E$ is used. The additive model assumes that all the components of the time series are independent of one another. For example, it is assumed that the long-term trend has no effect on the seasonal component no matter how low or how high this value may become.
11. These data are reported in *Year-Book of World Armament and Disarmament* (Stockholm: Stockholm Peace Research Institute, 1974).
12. For other methods, see Charles T. Clark and Lawrence L. Schkade, *Statistical Analysis for Administrative Decisions*, 2nd ed. (Cincinnati: South-Western, 1974), pp. 674–724.
13. For more exact techniques for testing for autocorrelation, see Frank, *Statistics and Econometrics*, pp. 273–283.

Chapter Six
Structural Equation Models

With regression analysis one can obtain quantitative assessments of relationships between two or more independent variables and a target variable. How changes in the values of the independent variables will affect the target variable can be estimated: regression coefficients tell how many units change in a target variable are obtained for each unit change in the program variables. In many situations, however, changes in some of the independent variables not only produce a change in the target variable but also affect other independent variables; that is, some of the independent variables might be causes of others. The existence of such causal sequences in real-life situations calls for the construction of impact models that represent such phenomena and are amenable to statistical analyses. Such multivariate models make use of entire sets of simultaneous equations, referred to as *structural systems*. This chapter deals with some of the basic issues involved in the construction of structural equation models and their application to policy evaluation research.

STRUCTURAL MODELS

After a number of variables have been delineated for inclusion in the impact model, a separate equation can be written for each as a possible dependent variable. Assuming that each of the variables in the impact model is caused by all of the remaining variables, and denoting the variables as $X_1, X_2, \ldots, X_k$, the following set of regression equations can be written:

$$X_1 = a_1 + b_{12}X_2 + b_{13}X_3 + \ldots + b_{1k}X_k + E_1$$
$$X_2 = a_2 + b_{21}X_1 + b_{23}X_3 + \ldots + b_{2k}X_k + E \qquad (6.1)$$

.

.

.

$$X_k = a_k + b_{k1}X_1 + b_{k2}X_2 + \ldots + b_{k,k-1}X_{k-1} + E_k$$

The E_is represent "disturbance terms." They refer to the effects of exogenous variables (variables not explicitly defined in the impact model) on the appropriate dependent variables. Note that $b_{12} \neq b_{21}$; whereas b_{12} stands for the regression coefficient when X_1 is taken as the dependent variable, b_{21} represents the regression coefficient when X_2 is taken as the dependent variable.

If the value of each of the independent variables in the system of equations is determined independently of the k dependent variables, the set of equations can be estimated by computing k single-equation ordinary least-square (OLS) regressions. However, if one or more of the k dependent variables are also independent variables in one or more of the equations, as in equation 6.1, the system of equations is termed a *simultaneous system*. The parameters of the structural equations in a simultaneous system of equations cannot be estimated by OLS because if, say, X_1 is estimated by X_2, the regression coefficient of the OLS regression of X_2 on X_1 is biased.[1] One procedure for obtaining estimates of the parameters of structural equations in a simultaneous system is the two-stage least-squares (2SLS) method, to be discussed later. The following section focuses on one subclass of simultaneous systems—recursive models.

RECURSIVE MODELS

A recursive model is one in which the direction of influence from any particular variable does not feed back to the variable either directly or indirectly. For example, there are four variables in the causal network shown in Figure 6.1; as indicated by the direction

Figure 6.1 **A Recursive Model**

of the arrows, X_1 is causally prior to X_2, which is causally prior to X_3, which is causally prior to X_4. There is no way to arrive back at any variable after leaving it without going against one of the arrows.

Recursive models do also cover cases in which one variable occurs at two distinct points in time, since the two measurements can be regarded as defining two different variables. For example, a model such as the one in Figure 6.2, where t and $t + 1$ are two periods of time, is recursive even though X appears to feed back upon itself.[2]

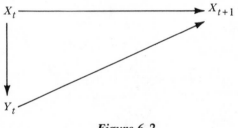

Figure 6.2

In terms of the system of equations, recursive models imply that some of the regression coefficients must be set equal to zero and that if $b_{ij} \neq 0$, then b_{ji} must equal zero. The general form of the set of equations can now be written:

$$X_1 = E_1$$
$$X_2 = b_{21}X_1 + E_2$$
$$X_3 = b_{31}X_1 + b_{32}X_2 + E_3 \quad (6.2)$$
$$\cdot$$
$$\cdot$$
$$\cdot$$
$$X_k = b_{k1}X_1 + b_{k2}X_2 + \ldots + b_{k,k-1}X_{k-1} + E_k$$

The constant terms have been eliminated by assuming that the variables are measured in terms of deviations from their respective means. Moreover, we are now taking X_1 to be an exogenous variable; its value is determined by variables outside the causal system. X_2, however, is affected not only by outside variables but also by X_1. X_3 is affected by X_1 and X_2 but not by any of the remaining variables in the impact model. Finally, X_k is affected by all the remaining X_is. The regression coefficients in recursive equation systems take on a triangular form, with half the bs set equal to zero.

Path Analysis

By introducing ratios of standard deviations (SD) into the form:

$$\frac{X_2}{SD_{X_2}} = b_{21} \frac{SD_{X_1}}{SD_{X_2}} \cdot \frac{X_1}{SD_{X_1}} + \frac{SD_E}{SD_{X_2}} \cdot \frac{E}{SD_E}$$

the expressions:

$$b_{21} \frac{SD_{X_1}}{SD_{X_2}} = p_{21}$$

$$\frac{SD_E}{SD_{X_2}} = p_{X_{2E}}$$

are obtained. These expressions are termed *path coefficients*. A path coefficient "measures the fraction of the standard deviations of the endogenous variable . . . for which the designated variable is directly responsible."[3] Thus the interpretation of path coefficients involves comparison of the relative magnitudes of the coefficients and assessment of how a specified change in one variable produces a change in another.

Expressed in terms of standardized values and path coefficients, the equation for a recursive model such as that shown in Figure 6.3 is:

$$X_2 = p_{21}X_1 + p_{2E}E \tag{6.3}$$

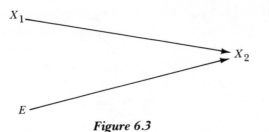

Figure 6.3

A four-variable recursive model can be explicitly represented by a path diagram such as that illustrated in Figure 6.4 and by a set of corresponding equations:

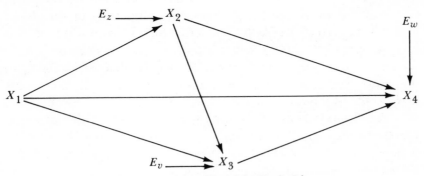

Figure 6.4   A Four-Variable Path Diagram

(X_1 exogenous)

$$X_2 = p_{21}X_1 + p_{2z}E_z$$

$$X_3 = p_{32}X_2 + p_{31}X_1 + p_{3v}E_v$$

$$X_4 = p_{43}X_3 + p_{42}X_2 + p_{41}X_1 + p_{4w}E_w$$

(6.4)

Note that in writing path coefficients the first numeral refers to the variable affected, the second to the causal variable. Accordingly, p_{21} stands for the path coefficient between X_2 and X_1, the latter representing the causal variable. In other words, a path coefficient measures the magnitude of a linkage between two or more variables. Graphically:

$$X_1 \xrightarrow{p_{21}} X_2$$

where X_1 is the causal variable. The E_is are residuals or disturbance terms; their estimation yields the residual path coefficient that provides a direct indication of the adequacy of the impact model. A cardinal assumption in recursive models is that the disturbance terms are uncorrelated with the independent variables (see chapter five). If the variables are in standard form, the system of equations can be solved using the OLS regression. For equation 6.4 this involves the regression of (1) X_2 on X_1, (2) X_3 on X_2 and X_1, and (3) X_4 on X_3, X_2, and X_1.

In addition to an overall estimation of impact models, path analysis allows the assessment of the direct and indirect effects that one variable has upon another. For example, in Figure 6.4, X_1 has a direct effect on X_4; X_1, however, also has indirect effects on X_4 via its effects on X_2 and X_3. Thus, the magnitude of the direct and indirect effects can be calculated, which helps in understanding the operative causal mechanisms of impact models.

One way to decompose the effects of path coefficients is to make use of the mathematical relations between path coefficients and product-moment coefficients. A basic statistical theorem states that the covariance of two standardized variables is the product-moment coefficient.[4] Accordingly, for a bivariate model (equation 6.3), we have an equality between the path coefficient and the correlation coefficient where:

$$r_{12} = p_{21}$$

The relationships between the correlation coefficients and the path coefficients for the model represented by equation 6.4 are expressed by the following set of equations:*

$$r_{12} = p_{21}$$
$$r_{13} = p_{31} + p_{32}p_{21}$$
$$r_{23} = p_{32} + p_{31}p_{21}$$
$$r_{14} = p_{41} + p_{42}p_{21} + p_{43}(p_{31} + p_{32}p_{21})$$
$$r_{24} = p_{42} + p_{43}p_{32} + p_{41}p_{21} + p_{43}p_{31}p_{21}$$
$$r_{34} = p_{43} + p_{42}(p_{32} + p_{31}p_{21}) + p_{41}(p_{31} + p_{32}p_{21})$$

(6.5)

* The general form for decomposition is $r_{ij} = \Sigma\, p_{ik}r_{jk}$, where i and j stand for any two variables in the system, and the index runs over all the variables from which paths lead directly to X_i.[5]

The entire correlation between X_1 and $X_2(r_{12})$ is generated by the direct effect p_{21}, as illustrated in Figure 6.5, where the bold arrow stands for the direct effect.

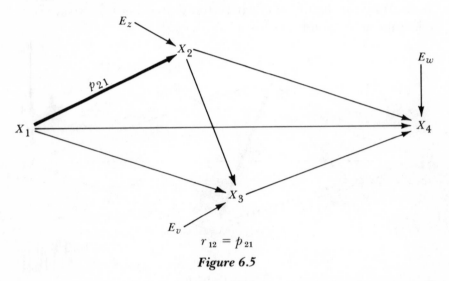

$$r_{12} = p_{21}$$

Figure 6.5

The correlation between X_1 and $X_3(r_{13})$ is produced by two distinct paths, so that r_{13} equals the direct effect p_{31} plus the indirect effect $p_{32}p_{21}$, as illustrated in Figure 6.6, where the dashed lines represent indirect effects.

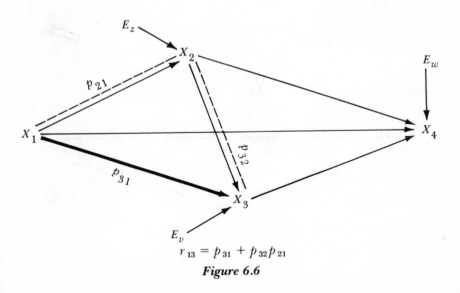

$$r_{13} = p_{31} + p_{32}p_{21}$$

Figure 6.6

The correlation between X_2 and $X_3(r_{23})$ is generated by a different mechanism: the total correlation equals the sum of the direct effect, p_{32}, plus correlation due to a common cause, $p_{31}p_{21}$, as illustrated in Figure 6.7, where the dotted lines stand for correlation due to common causes.

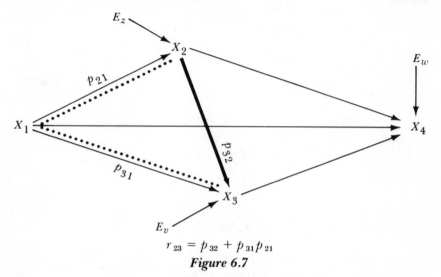

$$r_{23} = p_{32} + p_{31}p_{21}$$

Figure 6.7

As shown in Figure 6.8, the correlation between X_1 and $X_4(r_{14})$ is produced by four distinct causal links: r_{14} equals the direct effect,

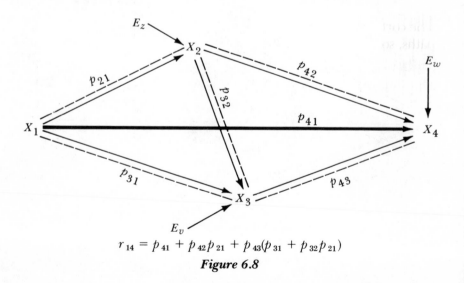

$$r_{14} = p_{41} + p_{42}p_{21} + p_{43}(p_{31} + p_{32}p_{21})$$

Figure 6.8

p_{41}, plus an indirect effect via X_2—$p_{42}p_{21}$—plus an indirect effect via X_3—$p_{43}p_{31}$—plus an indirect effect via X_3 and X_2——$p_{43}p_{32}p_{21}$.

A direct effect, an indirect effect, and correlation due to common causes are involved in generating r_{24}: r_{24} equals the direct effect, p_{42}, plus an indirect effect via X_3—$p_{43}p_{32}$—plus correlation due to X_1 operating as a common cause directly—$p_{41}p_{21}$—and indirectly (via X_3)—$p_{43}p_{31}p_{21}$:

$$r_{24} = p_{42} + p_{43}p_{32} + p_{41}p_{21} + p_{43}p_{31}p_{21}$$

There are no indirect effects in generating r_{34}; r_{34} equals the direct effect, p_{43}, plus correlation due to common causes, operating directly—$p_{42}p_{32}$ and $p_{41}p_{31}$—or indirectly—$p_{42}p_{31}p_{21}$ and $p_{41}p_{32}p_{21}$, as illustrated in Figure 6.9.

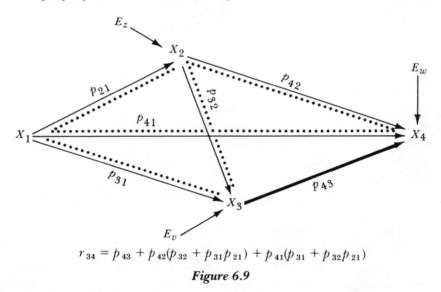

$$r_{34} = p_{43} + p_{42}(p_{32} + p_{31}p_{21}) + p_{41}(p_{31} + p_{32}p_{21})$$

Figure 6.9

In these and other cases, the correlation may be read off the path diagram using the multiplication rule: To find the correlation between X_i and X_j, where X_j appears later in the model, begin at X_j and read back to X_i along each distinct direct and indirect path, forming the product of the coefficients along that path. After reading back, read forward (if necessary); however, only one reversal from back to forward is permitted. The products obtained for all the paths between X_j and X_i are summed.[6]

Once the correlation coefficients are determined, the respective coefficients of determination (R^2) can be used to calculate the residual path coefficients. The general form of a residual path coefficient is:

$$\sqrt{1 - R^2} \tag{6.6}$$

The *residual path coefficient* is the square root of the unexplained variation in the dependent variable under analysis. For the model presented in Figure 6.4 and expressed by equation 6.4, the residual paths are:

$$p_{2z} = \sqrt{1 - R_{2(1)}^2}$$
$$p_{3v} = \sqrt{1 - R_{3(21)}^2}$$
$$p_{4w} = \sqrt{1 - R_{4(321)}^2}$$

One interesting application of path analysis is the Tompkins welfare expenditures model in the American states. Drawing on the theoretical literature, Gary L. Tompkins has constructed a recursive model that includes six variables: industrialization (X_1), income (X_2), ethnicity (X_3), interparty competition (X_4), voter turnout (X_5), and welfare expenditures (X_6).[7] Given the assumption of one-way causation, there are fifteen possible path arrows between the six variables, as illustrated in Figure 6.10. The values for the path coefficients and those for the residual paths are also reported in this figure.

The overall statistical explanatory power of this model can be evaluated with the coefficient of multiple correlation, $R = .838$. Although this path model accurately reflects the empirical relationships among the six variables, Tompkins has developed a more parsimonious model, obtained by eliminating weak path coefficients (coefficients with an absolute value less than .200) and then recalculating the various estimates. By eliminating six weak path coefficients, the more economical, but nonetheless powerful, model shown in Figure 6.11 was developed. The coefficient of multiple correlation for this model is $R = .831$, indicating that there is no substantial reduction in its explanatory power. Now it is possible to assess the direct and indirect effects of the variables on welfare expenditures. For example, ethnicity (measured as the percentage

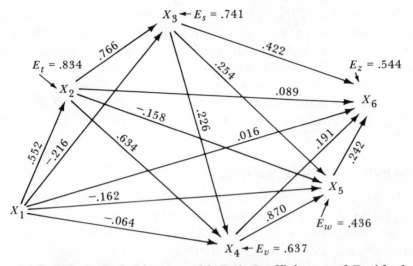

Figure 6.10   A Path Diagram with Path Coefficients and Residual Paths for Welfare Expenditures in the United States.

Source: Adapted from Gary L. Tompkins, "A Causal Model of State Welfare Expenditures," *Journal of Politics,* 37 (May 1975), 406, Fig. 3.

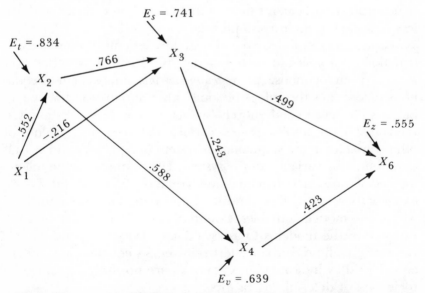

Figure 6.11   A Modified Path Diagram with Path Coefficients and Residual Paths for Welfare Expenditures in the United States.

Source: Adapted from Gary L. Tompkins, "A Causal Model of State Welfare Expenditures," *Journal of Politics,* 37 (May 1975), 409, Fig. 5.

of native born, of foreign, or of mixed parentage) exerts a strong direct effect on the level of welfare expenditures ($p_{63} = .499$) and a relatively moderate indirect effect via interparty competition: $p_{64} \cdot p_{43} = .102$. Income (measured as state per capita income) exerts no direct effect on welfare expenditures. However, income has a strong indirect effect via ethnicity and interparty competition: $(p_{63} \cdot p_{32}) + p_{64}[p_{42} + (p_{43} \cdot p_{32})] = (.499 \cdot .766) + .423[.588 + (.243 \cdot .766)] = .710$.

NONRECURSIVE MODELS

The recursive models discussed so far do not allow feedback loops or reciprocal linkages among the variables. Obviously this is a severe restriction on the kinds of impact models that can be quantitatively evaluated. In reality there are many instances in which one or more variables feed back into other variables. For instance, in the welfare expenditure model presented in Figure 6.10, one might expect that welfare expenditures would not only be affected by interparty competition but would themselves affect the extent to which parties are competitive. Such situations call for the construction of nonrecursive models that allow for feedback and are less restricted in their assumptions.

Nonrecursive models are expressed by systems of simultaneous equations. Variables in such systems are classified as either exogenous or endogenous. An *exogenous variable* in a system of equations determines the values of some other variables in the system but is itself determined entirely by factors outside the system. On the other hand, an *endogenous variable* determines the values of other variables in the simultaneous system of equations and is itself determined by variables in the system. For example, in the following set of simultaneous equations (equation 6.7), X_1 and X_2 are exogenous; their variance and their covariation are not explained within the model. Variables X_3 and X_4 are endogenous, and the purpose of the model is to assess their variations. E_3 and E_4 are, respectively, the disturbance terms in the X_3 equation and the X_4 equation; they indicate that X_3 and X_4 are not fully explained by their explicit determining factors.

$$X_3 = b_{31}X_1 + b_{34}X_4 + E_3$$
$$X_4 = b_{42}X_2 + b_{43}X_3 + E_4$$

$$(6.7)$$

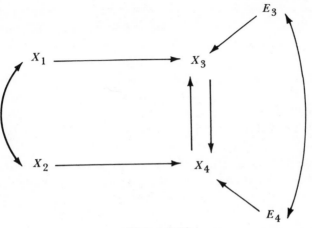

Figure 6.12

The causal mechanisms through which the exogenous variables determine the endogenous variables can be illustrated by a path diagram that represents these equations, as Figure 6.12 does for equation 6.7. Recall that in the recursive model it was assumed that disturbances are uncorrelated with exogenous variables. Nonrecursive models, as illustrated in Figure 6.12, do not require that the disturbances (or residual terms) be uncorrelated. This, in turn, is an important consideration that makes nonrecursive models more realistic for policy evaluation research. At the same time, the elimination of the noncorrelated disturbances assumption raises the problem of identification.

Identification
When an equation cannot be solved independently but has to be solved together with other equations in a simultaneous equation model, it often happens that two or more equations consisting of the same variables cannot be distinguished from one another. Since fewer restrictions are imposed in the nonrecursive model, there are more unknowns in the set of equations, and it thus becomes more difficult to obtain unique solutions. In other words, the problem of identification is that of having sufficient information to obtain unique solutions for a set of unknowns.

Consider the equations:

$$X + Y = 3$$
$$X - Y = 1$$

A unique solution is a pair (X, Y) of real numbers that simultaneously make both equations correct statements. The unique solution of this system is $X = 2$, $Y = 1$. We simply added the equations; the Y drops out and $2X = 4$, so $X = 2$. Now, $X + Y = 3$, $2 + Y = 3$, so $Y = 1$. The only possible solution of the preceding system is $X = 2$, $Y = 1$. Such a system of equations represents an exactly identified system since there are just as many independent equations as unknowns; the information is sufficient to obtain a unique solution.

A system of simultaneous equations is considered underidentified when there are fewer independent equations than unknowns. For example, a system such as:

$$X + Y + Z = 1$$
$$X - 2Y + 2Z = 4$$
$$2X - Y + 3Z = 5$$

is underidentified because it has no unique solution but a family of solutions. If we eliminate X from the second and third equations, then:

$$X + Y + Z = 1$$
$$-3Y + Z = 3$$
$$-3Y + Z = 3$$

However, the last two equations convey the same information. Therefore, the system is equivalent to the system:

$$X + Y + Z = 1$$
$$-3Y + Z = 3$$

Such a system has no one solution, and is regarded as an underidentified system of equations.

When there are more equations than unknowns the system of equations is referred to as an overidentified system. For instance, a system such as:

$$2Y - X = 5$$
$$Y + 3X = 0$$
$$3Y - 2X = 3$$

is overidentified because the solution of different pairs of equations would give dissimilar results. If we used the first and second equations to solve the system, we would obtain $X = -5/7$; if we used the first and third equations, we would obtain $X = 9$; and if we used the second and third equations, then $X = -3/11$. Even though different pairs of equations give different results, there is one finite set of solutions for overidentified systems.

To estimate the parameters (regression coefficients and/or path coefficients) of simultaneous equation models, one must first determine whether any particular system is exactly identified, overidentified, or underidentified. In recursive models the assumptions about error terms guarantee that the system of equations is at least exactly identified.[8] Furthermore, at least half the coefficients are equal to zero: if it is postulated that, say, X_1 causes X_2 (represented by p_{21}), then p_{12} must equal zero. Consequently, unique solutions are generated, and the OLS regression yields consistent and unbiased estimates of the equations' parameters. In nonrecursive models fewer restrictions are made on the coefficients and the residual terms, thereby leading to more unknowns and greater difficulties in obtaining unique solutions. Relatedly, the OLS is an inadequate estimator in nonrecursive models because the estimates are inconsistent as well as biased.

Two conditions are involved with identification—the order condition and the rank condition. The order condition states that a necessary condition for the identifiability of a structural equation in a given system of simultaneous equations is that the number of variables excluded from the equation be at least equal to the number (K, say) of structural equations less one. When the structural equations are written with the dependent variable isolated on the left side of the expression, an equivalent version of the order condition states that "the number of exogenous variables excluded from the equation must at least equal the number of endogenous variables included on the right-hand side of the equation."[9] A necessary and sufficient condition for the identifiability of a structural equation is that at least one nonzero determinant[10] of order $K - 1$ can be formed out of those coefficients with which the variables excluded from that structural equation appear in the other $K - 1$ structural equations. This is known as the rank condition of identifiability. If two or more nonzero determinants can be found, then the equation in question is overidentified.[11]

Estimation

The order and rank conditions help in determining whether the equations are underidentified, exactly identified, or overidentified. The next problem is how to obtain estimates of the unknown coefficients for each category of identification.

Underidentification   When an equation is underidentified, there is no estimation technique that yields satisfactory estimates. OLS, for example, would produce biased and inconsistent estimates. In practice, attempts are made to convert an underidentified equation to an identified one by introducing new variables into the model; such variables are referred to as *instrumental variables*. Although substantive considerations play a major role in the search for in-

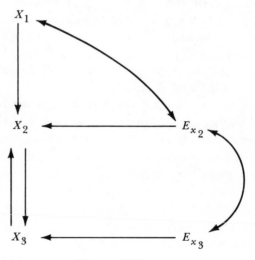

Figure 6.13

strumental variables to be included in the impact model, such variables should also exhibit certain statistical properties.

Formally, a variable X_1 is an instrument for X_2 in a nonrecursive relationship $X_2 \rightarrow X_3$ if (1) X_1 has no direct effect on X_3; (2) X_1 does affect X_2 either directly or indirectly through a variable that has no direct effect on X_3; (3) neither X_2 nor X_3 has a direct or indirect effect on X_1; (4) no disturbance term jointly affects X_1 and X_3, and, in general, X_1 is uncorrelated with the disturbances of X_3.[12] For example, in Figure 6.13, X_1 is a valid instrumental variable relative to the relation $X_2 \rightarrow X_3$. The relationship between X_1 and X_3 is like a recursive relationship since X_3 has no effect on X_1 and X_1 is uncorrelated with the residual terms affecting $X_3(E_{X_3})$. On the other hand, X_1 is unlike an ordinary recursive variable because it must not have a direct effect on X_3; it must influence X_3 only through other specified variables, and in particular through X_2.

A variable may serve as an instrumental variable for more than one relationship, as illustrated in Figure 6.14, where Z is an in-

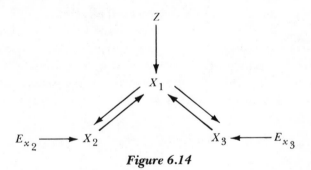

Figure 6.14

strument for $X_1 \rightarrow X_2$ and for $X_1 \rightarrow X_3$. Instrumental variables provide necessary information for identification. However, as Lawrence R. Klein has suggested, "Identification cannot be cheaply achieved in any particular investigation by simply adding some weak or marginal variable to one of the relationships of a system. One must add something substantial and significant which had been previously neglected."[13]

Exact Identification When the nonrecursive system is identified, a number of estimation methods can be used. One general method of estimating parameters in nonrecursive models is the *two-stage least-squares* (2SLS) technique,[14] a procedure for obtaining the coefficients of structural equations in exactly identified or overidentified simultaneous systems of equations.

Suppose the two structural equations are:

I. $\qquad Y_1 = a_0 + a_1Y_2 + a_2X_1 + a_3X_2 + a_4X_3 + E_1$

II. $\qquad Y_2 = b_0 + b_1Y_1 + b_2X_1 + b_3X_4 + E_2$

where X_1, X_2, X_3, and X_4 are the exogenous variables; a and b designate the coefficients; and E_1 and E_2 are disturbances or error terms. The slope coefficient of Y_2 in Equation I, computed from a single-equation OLS regression, is subject to bias because Y_2 and Y_1 influence each other (nonrecursive relation). Equation I could be estimated if Y_2 were cleansed of the effect of Y_1 on Y_2. This can be accomplished by using a predicted $\hat{Y}_2$ rather than the observed Y_2, assuming that the predicted $\hat{Y}_2$ is statistically independent of Y_1.

The first stage in the 2SLS procedure is the calculation of the OLS regression of Y_2 on all the exogenous variables in the system. The obtained equation is referred to as the reduced-form equation for Y_2. In the reduced-form equation the exogenous variables are determined independently of Y_2 and Y_1, and thus are not subject to bias. The reduced-form equation for Y_2 is expressed as:

$$\hat{Y}_2 = \pi_0 + \pi_1X_1 + \pi_2X_2 + \pi_3X_3 + \pi_4X_4 + \text{E}$$

where the πs are the reduced-form equation coefficients and E is a disturbance term. The observed values of the exogenous variables are inserted into the computed reduced-form equation to obtain predicted values for $\hat{Y}_2$. The predicted values of $\hat{Y}_2$ are then used as the Y_2 data in Equation I, and the OLS regression for Equation I is computed.

The second-stage equation is:

$$\hat{\hat{Y}}_1 = a_0 + a_1\hat{Y}_2 + a_2X_1 + a_3X_2 + a_4X_3 + \hat{E}_1$$

where $\hat{\hat{Y}}$ denotes 2SLS estimates. A similar analysis is performed for Equation II. The reduced-form equation (first-stage regression) is:

$$\hat{Y}_1 = \pi_0' + \pi_1'X_1 + \pi_2'X_2 + \pi_3'X_3 + \pi_4'X_4 + \acute{E}$$

The predicted values for $\hat{Y}_1$ are obtained by inserting the observed values of the exogenous variables into the reduced-form equation. The coefficients of Equation II are then obtained from the regression of Y_2 on predicted $\hat{Y}_1$ and the exogenous variables in Equation II:

$$\hat{\hat{Y}}_2 = b_0 + b_1\hat{Y}_1 + b_2X_1 + b_3X_4 + \hat{E}_2$$

For large samples the coefficient a_1 is an unbiased estimate of the effect of Y_2 on Y_1 in Equation I, and b_1 is an unbiased estimate of the relation between Y_1 and Y_2 in Equation II.*

Before proceeding to a detailed illustration of the use of 2SLS, the idea of a reduced-form equation calls for further explication. Essentially, a reduced-form equation expresses one endogenous variable as a function of the exogenous variables in the impact model. In a system of equations, one reduced-form equation is written for each endogenous variable. Thus, with h endogenous variables, $Y_1, \ldots, Y_h$, and k exogenous variables, $X_1, \ldots, X_k$, the system of equations may be written in the general form as:

$$Y_1 = b_{12}Y_2 + \ldots + b_{1h}Y_{1h} + c_{11}X_1 + \ldots + c_{1k}X_k + E_1$$

.

.

(6.8)

.

$$Y_h = b_{h1}Y_1 + \ldots + b_{h,h-1}Y_{h-1} + c_{h1}X_1 + \ldots + c_{hk}X_k + E_h$$

This system of equations can be further expressed as a set of linear equations for the h variables $Y_1, \ldots, Y_h$ and written as

* The coefficients a_1 and b_1 are consistent estimates of the population coefficients α_1 and β_1.

linear functions of the variables $X_1, \ldots, X_k$:

$$Y_1 = \pi_{11}X_1 + \ldots + \pi_{1k}X_k + E_1$$

.

.   (6.9)

.

$$Y_h = \pi_{h1}X_1 + \ldots + \pi_{hk}X_k + E_h$$

where the disturbance terms E_i are linear functions of the E_i, and both coefficients π_{ij} and errors E_i are functions of the coefficients b_{ij} and π_{ij}. Equation 6.9 is termed the *reduced form* of the equation system, and the hk coefficients π_{ij} are termed *reduced-form coefficients*. By successively regressing $Y_1, \ldots, Y_h$ on $X_1, \ldots, X_k$ together, least-squares estimates of the reduced-form coefficients can be obtained.

Robert Mason and Albert N. Halter applied the 2SLS procedure to estimate an innovation-diffusion model of considerable relevance to policy evaluation research.[15] The model consists of four endogenous and seven exogenous variables. The endogenous variables are: Y_1—social influence; Y_2—prestige; Y_3—innovation-adoption; and Y_4—level of production. The expected causal relations between these variables can be specified as:

$$Y_1 \leftarrow (Y_2, Y_4)$$
$$Y_2 \leftarrow (Y_1, Y_4)$$
$$Y_3 \leftarrow (Y_1, Y_2)$$
$$Y_4 \leftarrow (Y_3)$$

It can be seen that social influence is hypothesized to be caused by prestige and level of production, and prestige, in turn, by social influence and also by level of production. Innovation-adoption is predicted to be caused by social influence and prestige, and level of production is postulated to be caused by innovation-adoption.

The seven exogenous variables are assumed to be outside the interdependent system. The variables are: X_1—type of residence; X_2—formal education; X_3—age; X_4—control over production resources; X_5—exposure to mass media appropriate for the exercise of influence; X_6—use of technological information sources; and X_7—exposure to mass media appropriate for recognition.* Combined with the causal relationships postulated among the endogenous variables, the complete system of hypothesized relationships is:

$$Y_1 \leftarrow (Y_2, Y_4; X_2, X_4, X_5)$$
$$Y_2 \leftarrow (Y_1, Y_4; X_1, X_2, X_7)$$
$$Y_3 \leftarrow (Y_1, Y_2; X_6)$$
$$Y_4 \leftarrow (Y_3; X_1, X_3, X_4)$$

This system is illustrated by the arrow-diagram in Figure 6.15.

For the purpose of estimation, the system of equations can be written as:

$$Y_1 = c_1 + a_{11}Y_2 + a_{12}Y_4 + b_{11}X_2 + b_{12}X_4 + b_{13}X_5 + E_1$$
$$Y_2 = c_2 + a_{21}Y_1 + a_{22}Y_4 + b_{21}X_1 + b_{22}X_2 + b_{23}X_7 + E_2$$
$$Y_3 = c_3 + a_{31}Y_1 + a_{32}Y_2 + b_{31}X_6 + E_3$$
$$Y_4 = c_4 + a_{41}Y_3 + b_{41}X_1 - b_{42}X_3 + b_{43}X_4 + E_4$$

This system is then transformed into reduced-form equations:

$$\hat{Y}_1 = \pi_1 + z_{11}X_1 + z_{12}X_2 - z_{13}X_3 + z_{14}X_4 + z_{15}X_5 + z_{16}X_6 + z_{17}X_7 + \acute{E}_1$$
$$\hat{Y}_2 = \pi_2 + z_{21}X_1 + z_{22}X_2 - z_{23}X_3 + z_{24}X_4 + z_{25}X_5 + z_{26}X_6 + z_{27}X_7 + \acute{E}_2$$
$$\hat{Y}_3 = \pi_3 + z_{31}X_1 + z_{32}X_2 - z_{33}X_3 + z_{34}X_4 + z_{35}X_5 + z_{36}X_6 + z_{37}X_7 + \acute{E}_3$$
$$\hat{Y}_4 = \pi_4 + z_{41}X_1 + z_{42}X_2 - z_{43}X_3 + z_{44}X_4 + z_{45}X_5 + z_{46}X_6 + z_{47}X_7 + \acute{E}_4$$

where each endogenous variable ($\hat{Y}_i$) is written as a function of all the exogenous variables (X_1 to X_7). Since each equation now contains only one endogenous variable, the coefficients in each equation can be estimated by OLS regression. This is the first stage of the 2SLS procedure.

The next step is to obtain estimated values for the endogenous

---

* These as well as the endogenous variables were measured at the individual level.

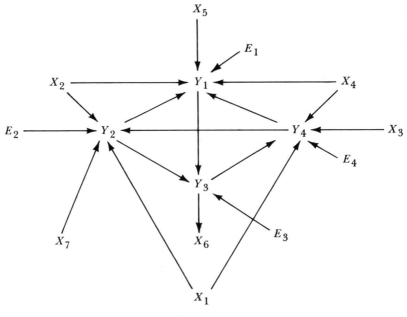

Figure 6.15

variables using these coefficients and the observed values for the exogenous variables. Using these new values of the endogenous variables, $\hat{Y}_1$, $\hat{Y}_2$, $\hat{Y}_3$, $\hat{Y}_4$, and the same observed values of the exogenous variables on the right-hand side, one then estimates the coefficients in the original system by OLS regression. In other words, each equation is estimated separately in the following system:

$$\hat{Y}_1 = c_1 + a_{11}\hat{Y}_2 + a_{12}\hat{Y}_4 + b_{11}X_2 + b_{12}X_4 + b_{13}X_5 + \acute{E}_1$$

$$\hat{Y}_2 = c_2 + a_{21}\hat{Y}_1 + a_{22}\hat{Y}_4 + b_{21}X_1 + b_{22}X_2 + b_{23}X_7 + \acute{E}_2$$

$$\hat{Y}_3 = c_3 + a_{31}\hat{Y}_1 + a_{32}\hat{Y}_2 + b_{31}X_6 + \acute{E}_3$$

$$\hat{Y}_4 = c_4 + a_{41}\hat{Y}_3 + b_{41}X_1 - b_{42}X_3 + b_{43}X_4 + \acute{E}_4$$

The structural form of the model with the estimated coefficients obtained by the 2SLS technique are:

$$\hat{\hat{Y}}_1 = -4.239 + (.315)\hat{Y}_2 + (.514 \times 10^{-5})\hat{Y}_4$$
$$+ (.063)X_2 - (.950 \times 10^{-3})X_4 + (.409)X_5$$
$$(ns)*$$

$$\hat{\hat{Y}}_2 = 31.423 + (1.558)\hat{Y}_1 - (.321 \times 10^{-5})\hat{Y}_4$$
$$- (.877 \times 10^{-4})X_1 + (.060)X_2 + (.467)X_7$$
$$(ns) \qquad\qquad (ns)$$

$$\hat{\hat{Y}}_3 = -.588 + (.185)\hat{Y}_1 - (.023)\hat{Y}_2 + (.047)X_6$$
$$(ns)$$

$$\hat{\hat{Y}}_4 = 103705.4 + (92887.6)\hat{Y}_3 + (5.696)X_1$$
$$- (1714.8)X_3 + (371.12)X_4$$

The first equation indicates that whereas prestige, production, education, and exposure to mass media appropriate for the exercise of influence** are significantly related to social influence, control over production resources (X_4) does not affect social influence. This in turn suggests that the basis for social influence is production, not control of resources. The second equation shows that social influence as well as exposure to mass media appropriate for recognition† significantly affect prestige. Production, type of residence, and education do not exert a significant impact on prestige. But although education does not have a direct effect on prestige, it is a predictor of social influence, and social influence is in turn a predictor of prestige. In the third equation, social influence and use of technological information sources influence innovation-adoption $(\hat{Y}_3)$, whereas prestige does not. However, prestige serves as a base for social influence, which in turn is related to innovation-adoption. In the last equation, innovation-adoption,

* The expression (ns) under some coefficients indicates that the coefficient is not statistically significant when the t-test is applied.
** This variable was measured by the number of specialized magazine subscriptions.
† This variable was measured by the number of weekly newspaper subscriptions.

type of residence, and control over production resources are all significantly related to production.

Summarizing the substantive implications of their study, Mason and Halter observe:

> [Influential individuals] adopt significant innovations which contribute, in turn, to increased production. Decision leading to the adoption of innovations may require considerable information from many sources, including the mass media. While influentials may (or may not) pass on information to those who are less influential, there is a considerable evidence which suggests that this information is used for the pursuit of purely economic goals. Thus, influentials appear to play a key role in the agricultural production process, a role distinct—but not independent—from their prestige and other attributes of social position. The fact that they are more productive . . . enhances their influence position and undoubtedly has implications for their capital position as well.[16]

Overidentification   When the nonrecursive system of simultaneous equations is overidentified, the 2SLS procedure is one appropriate method for estimating the coefficients. Other procedures, such as full-information methods, are more complex and can be described only by using a higher level of mathematics.[17]

The basics of structural equation models have now been set out. Many important topics have merely been introduced, while others have not been presented at all. Problems such as nonadditive relationships, the use of dummy variables for nominal and ordinal data, and nonrandom measurement errors are important topics but beyond the scope of this book.[18] Essentially, I have attempted to convey the potential of structural equation models for policy evaluation research, inasmuch as they present one of the most promising and powerful methodologies for clarifying and testing our thinking about the consequences of public policies.

NOTES

1. For the mathematical proof see, for example, Jan Kmenta, *Elements of Econometrics* (New York: Macmillan, 1971), pp. 297–304.
2. Otis Dudley Duncan, *Introduction to Structural Equation Models* (New York: Academic Press, 1975), pp. 25–28.

3. Kenneth C. Land, "Principles of Path Analysis," in Edgar Borgatta, ed., *Sociological Methodology 1969* (San Francisco: Jossey-Bass, 1969), pp. 8–9.

4. A standardized variable has a zero mean and a unit variance.

5. For the derivation of this basic theorem, see Otis Dudley Duncan, "Path Analysis: Sociological Samples," in Hubert M. Blalock, Jr., ed., *Causal Models in the Social Sciences* (Chicago: Aldine, 1971), pp. 114–123.

6. Duncan, *Introduction to Structural Equation Models*, p. 36.

7. Gary L. Tompkins, "A Causal Model of State Welfare Expenditures," *Journal of Politics*, 37 (May 1975), 392–416.

8. Raymond Boudon, "A New Look at Correlation Analysis," in Hubert M. Blalock, Jr., and Ann B. Blalock, eds., *Methodology in Social Research* (New York: McGraw-Hill, 1968), p. 205.

9. Ronald J. Wonnacott and Thomas H. Wonnacott, *Econometrics* (New York: Wiley, 1970), p. 180.

10. A *matrix* is a rectangle of numbers. Associated with the system of equations:

$$3X + Y - 2Z = 4$$

$$-5X \quad + 2Z = 5$$

$$-7X - Y + 3Z = -2$$

is the matrix:

$$\begin{bmatrix} 3 & 1 & -2 & : & 4 \\ -5 & 0 & 2 & : & 5 \\ -7 & -1 & 3 & : & -2 \end{bmatrix}$$

This is a 3×4 matrix (3 rows and 4 columns). The dotted line separates the coefficients of the unknowns from the constants. Associated with any square ($n \times n$) matrix is a scalar quantity called a *determinant*. For a 2×2 matrix:

$$\begin{bmatrix} a & b \\ c & d \end{bmatrix}$$

we define the determinant by:

$$det \begin{bmatrix} a & b \\ c & d \end{bmatrix} = ad - bc$$

The determinant of a 3×3 matrix is a number, defined by:

$$\begin{bmatrix} a_1 & b_1 & c_1 \\ a_2 & b_2 & c_2 \\ a_3 & b_3 & c_3 \end{bmatrix} = a_1 b_2 c_3 + a_2 b_3 c_1 + a_3 b_1 c_2 - a_1 b_3 c_2 - a_2 b_1 c_3 - a_3 b_2 c_1$$

Evaluation of determinants of higher order than 3 × 3 is straightforward. The presence of a nonzero determinant indicates that there is a unique solution, whereas a zero determinant indicates that there is no such solution. For a more detailed discussion of matrix algebra as applied to structural equation models, see Gordon Hilton, *Intermediate Politometrics* (New York: Columbia University Press, 1976), chap. 6.

11. For a more detailed and nontechnical discussion of the order and rank conditions, see Herbert B. Asher, *Causal Modeling,* Sage University Papers No. 3 (Beverly Hills, Calif.: Sage, 1976), pp. 52–54.
12. David R. Heise, *Causal Analysis* (New York: Wiley-Interscience, 1975), pp. 160–161.
13. Lawrence R. Klein, *An Introduction to Econometrics* (Englewood Cliffs, N.J.: Prentice-Hall, 1962), p. 18.
14. Another technique is the indirect least squares. See, for example, Charles R. Frank, Jr., *Statistics and Econometrics* (New York: Holt, Rinehart & Winston, 1971), pp. 310–315.
15. Robert Mason and Albert N. Halter, "The Application of a System of Simultaneous Equations to an Innovation Diffusion Model," *Social Forces,* 47 (December 1968), 182–195.
16. Ibid., pp. 194–195.
17. See, for example, Karl A. Fox, *Intermediate Economic Statistics* (New York: Wiley, 1968), chaps. 11 and 12.
18. See Duncan, *Introduction to Structural Equation Models*; Heise, *Causal Analysis*; and N. Krishnan Namboodiri, Lewis F. Carter, and Hubert M. Blalock, Jr., *Applied Multivariate Analysis and Experimental Designs* (New York: McGraw-Hill, 1975).

APPENDIXES
BIBLIOGRAPHY
INDEX

Appendix A   The Standard Normal Distribution

z	.00	.01	.02	.03	.04	.05	.06	.07	.08	.09
0.0	.0000	.0040	.0080	.0120	.0160	.0199	.0239	.0279	.0319	.0359
0.1	.0398	.0438	.0478	.0517	.0557	.0596	.0636	.0675	.0714	.0753
0.2	.0793	.0832	.0871	.0910	.0948	.0987	.1026	.1064	.1103	.1141
0.3	.1179	.1217	.1255	.1293	.1331	.1368	.1406	.1443	.1480	.1517
0.4	.1554	.1591	.1628	.1664	.1700	.1736	.1772	.1808	.1844	.1879
0.5	.1915	.1950	.1985	.2019	.2054	.2088	.2123	.2157	.2190	.2224
0.6	.2257	.2291	.2324	.2357	.2389	.2422	.2454	.2486	.2517	.2549
0.7	.2580	.2611	.2642	.2673	.2704	.2734	.2764	.2794	.2823	.2852
0.8	.2881	.2910	.2939	.2967	.2995	.3023	.3051	.3078	.3106	.3133
0.9	.3159	.3186	.3212	.3238	.3264	.3289	.3315	.3340	.3365	.3389
1.0	.3413	.3438	.3461	.3485	.3508	.3531	.3554	.3577	.3599	.3621
1.1	.3643	.3665	.3686	.3708	.3729	.3749	.3770	.3790	.3810	.3830
1.2	.3849	.3869	.3888	.3907	.3925	.3944	.3962	.3980	.3997	.4015
1.3	.4032	.4049	.4066	.4082	.4099	.4115	.4131	.4147	.4162	.4177
1.4	.4192	.4207	.4222	.4236	.4251	.4265	.4279	.4292	.4306	.4319
1.5	.4332	.4345	.4357	.4370	.4382	.4394	.4406	.4418	.4429	.4441
1.6	.4452	.4463	.4474	.4484	.4495	.4505	.4515	.4525	.4535	.4545
1.7	.4554	.4564	.4573	.4582	.4591	.4599	.4608	.4616	.4625	.4633
1.8	.4641	.4649	.4656	.4664	.4671	.4678	.4686	.4693	.4699	.4706
1.9	.4713	.4719	.4726	.4732	.4738	.4744	.4750	.4756	.4761	.4767
2.0	.4772	.4778	.4783	.4788	.4793	.4798	.4803	.4808	.4812	.4817
2.1	.4821	.4826	.4830	.4834	.4838	.4842	.4846	.4850	.4854	.4857
2.2	.4861	.4864	.4868	.4871	.4875	.4878	.4881	.4884	.4887	.4890
2.3	.4893	.4896	.4898	.4901	.4904	.4906	.4909	.4911	.4913	.4916
2.4	.4918	.4920	.4922	.4925	.4927	.4929	.4931	.4932	.4934	.4936
2.5	.4938	.4940	.4941	.4943	.4945	.4946	.4948	.4949	.4951	.4952
2.6	.4953	.4955	.4956	.4957	.4959	.4960	.4961	.4962	.4963	.4964
2.7	.4965	.4966	.4967	.4968	.4969	.4970	.4971	.4972	.4973	.4974
2.8	.4974	.4975	.4976	.4977	.4977	.4978	.4979	.4979	.4980	.4981
2.9	.4981	.4982	.4982	.4983	.4984	.4984	.4985	.4985	.4986	.4986
3.0	.4987	.4987	.4987	.4988	.4988	.4989	.4989	.4989	.4990	.4990

Source: Harold O. Rugg, *Statistical Methods Applied to Education* (Boston: Houghton Mifflin, 1917), appendix table III, pp. 389–390. Reprinted with the kind permission of the publisher.

Appendix B The *t* Distribution

	LEVEL OF SIGNIFICANCE FOR ONE-TAILED TEST					
	.10	.05	.025	.01	.005	.0005
	LEVEL OF SIGNIFICANCE FOR TWO-TAILED TEST					
df	.20	.10	.05	.02	.01	.001
1	3.078	6.314	12.706	31.821	63.657	636.619
2	1.886	2.920	4.303	6.965	9.925	31.598
3	1.638	2.353	3.182	4.541	5.841	12.941
4	1.533	2.132	2.776	3.747	4.604	8.610
5	1.476	2.015	2.571	3.365	4.032	6.859
6	1.440	1.943	2.447	3.143	3.707	5.959
7	1.415	1.895	2.365	2.998	3.499	5.405
8	1.397	1.860	2.306	2.896	3.355	5.041
9	1.383	1.833	2.262	2.821	3.250	4.781
10	1.372	1.812	2.228	2.764	3.169	4.587
11	1.363	1.796	2.201	2.718	3.106	4.437
12	1.356	1.782	2.179	2.681	3.055	4.318
13	1.350	1.771	2.160	2.650	3.012	4.221
14	1.345	1.761	2.145	2.624	2.977	4.140
15	1.341	1.753	2.131	2.602	2.947	4.073
16	1.337	1.746	2.120	2.583	2.921	4.015
17	1.333	1.740	2.110	2.567	2.898	3.965
18	1.330	1.734	2.101	2.552	2.878	3.922
19	1.328	1.729	2.093	2.539	2.861	3.883
20	1.325	1.725	2.086	2.528	2.845	3.850
21	1.323	1.721	2.080	2.518	2.831	3.819
22	1.321	1.717	2.074	2.508	2.819	3.792
23	1.319	1.714	2.069	2.500	2.807	3.767
24	1.318	1.711	2.064	2.492	2.797	3.745
25	1.316	1.708	2.060	2.485	2.787	3.725
26	1.315	1.706	2.056	2.479	2.779	3.707
27	1.314	1.703	2.052	2.473	2.771	3.690
28	1.313	1.701	2.048	2.467	2.763	3.674
29	1.311	1.699	2.045	2.462	2.756	3.659
30	1.310	1.697	2.042	2.457	2.750	3.646
40	1.303	1.684	2.021	2.423	2.704	3.551
60	1.296	1.671	2.000	2.390	2.660	3.460
120	1.289	1.658	1.980	2.358	2.617	3.373
∞	1.282	1.645	1.960	2.326	2.576	3.291

Source: This table is taken from Table III of R. A. Fisher and F. Yates, *Statistical Tables for Biological, Agricultural and Medical Research,* published by Longman Group Ltd., London (previously published by Oliver and Boyd, Edinburgh), and by permission of the authors and publishers.

A Selected Bibliography

This bibliography is intended to provide reference material for those interested in pursuing further the issues raised in this book.

Abt, Clark C. (ed.). *The Evaluation of Social Programs*. Beverly Hills, Calif.: Sage, 1976.

Ackoff, Russell L. *Scientific Method: Optimizing Applied Research Decisions*. New York: Wiley, 1962.

Alkin, Marvin C. "Evaluation Theory Development." *Evaluation Comment*, 2 (October 1969), 2–7.

American Institutes for Research. *Evaluative Research Strategies and Methods*. Pittsburgh, Pa.: American Institutes for Research, 1970.

Anderson, James C. "Causal Model of Health Services Systems." *Health Services Research*, 7 (Spring 1972), 23–42.

Anderson, James E. *Public Policy-Making*. New York: Praeger, 1975.

Anderson, James G., and Francis B. Evans. "Causal Models in Educational Research: Recursive Models." *American Educational Research Journal*, 11 (Winter 1974), 29–39.

Apple, Michael W., Michael J. Subkoviak, and Henry S. Lufler, Jr. (eds.). *Education Evaluation: Analysis and Responsibility*. Berkeley, Calif.: McCutchan, 1974.

Archibald, K. A. "Three Views on the Expert's Role in Policymaking: Systems Analysis, Incrementalism, and the Clinical Approach." *Policy Sciences*, 1 (Spring 1970), 73–86.

Asher, Herbert B. *Causal Modeling*. Sage University Papers No. 3. Beverly Hills, Calif.: Sage, 1976.

Baldus, David C. "Welfare as a Loan: An Empirical Study of the Recovery of Public Assistance Payments in the United States." *Stanford Law Review*, 25 (January 1973), 123–250.

Barber, Bernard, et al. *Research on Human Subjects*. New York: Russell Sage Foundation, 1973.

Bardach, Eugene. *The Implementation Game: What Happens After a Bill Becomes a Law*. Cambridge, Mass.: M.I.T. Press, 1977.

Bateman, Worth. "Assessing Program Effectiveness: A Rating System for Identifying Relative Project Success." *Welfare in Review*, 6 (January–February 1968), 1–10.

Beightler, Charles S., and Velna Rae Thurman. "Management Science Models for Evaluating Regional Government Policies." *Omega*, 3 (February 1975), 71–78.

Bennis, Warren, Kenneth D. Benne, and Robert Chin (eds.). *The Planning of Change*. 2nd ed. New York: Holt, Rinehart & Winston, 1969.

Berlak, Harold. "Values, Goals, Public Policy and Educational Evaluation." *Review of Educational Research*, 40 (April 1970), 261–278.

Berleman, William C., and Thomas W. Steinburn. "The Execution and Evaluation of a Delinquency Prevention Program." *Social Problems*, 14 (Spring 1967), 413–423.

Bernstein, Ilene N. (ed.). *Validity Issues in Evaluative Research*. Sage Contemporary Social Science Issues, XXIII. Beverly Hills, Calif.: Sage, 1976.

————, and Howard E. Freeman. *Academic and Entrepreneurial Research*. New York: Russell Sage Foundation, 1975.

Bhattacharyya, Gouri K., and Richard A. Johnson. *Statistical Concepts and Methods*. New York: Wiley, 1977.

Bisco, Ralph L. (ed.). *Data Banks, Computers and the Social Sciences*. New York: Wiley-Interscience, 1970.

Blalock, Hubert M., Jr. *Causal Inferences in Nonexperimental Research*. Chapel Hill: University of North Carolina Press, 1964.

————. *Theory Construction*. Englewood Cliffs, N.J.: Prentice-Hall, 1969.

———— (ed.). *Causal Models in the Social Sciences*. Chicago: Aldine, 1971.

————. *Quantitative Sociology: International Perspectives on Mathematical and Statistical Modeling*. New York: Academic Press, 1975.

————, and Ann B. Blalock (eds.). *Methodology in Social Research*. New York: McGraw-Hill, 1968.

Blum, Henrik. "Evaluating Health Care." *Medical Care*, 12 (December 1974), 999–1011.

Borgatta, Edgar. "Research Problems in Evaluation of Health Service Demonstrations." *Milbank Memorial Fund Quarterly*, 44 (October 1966), Part 2, 182–201.

Boruch, Robert F. "Problems in Research Utilization: Use of Social Experiments, Experimental Results and Auxiliary Data in Experiments." *Annals of the New York Academy of Sciences*, 218 (June 1973), 56–77.

————. "Relations Among Statistical Methods for Assuring Confidentiality of Data." *Social Science Research*, 1 (December 1972), 403–414.

Borus, Michael E. (ed.). *Evaluating the Impact of Manpower Programs*. Lexington, Mass.: Lexington Books, 1972.

————, and William R. Tash. *Measuring the Impact of Manpower Programs: A Primer*. Policy Papers in Human Resources and Industrial Relations, No. 17. Ann Arbor, Mich.: Institute of Labor and Industrial Relations, 1970.

Box, George E. P., and Gwilyn M. Jenkins. *Time-Series Analysis: Forecasting and Control*. San Francisco: Holden-Day, 1970.

Brewer, Garry D. *Politicians, Bureaucrats and the Consultant*. New York: Basic Books, 1973.

Brown, Richard, and Ray D. Pethtel. "A Matter of Facts: State Legislative Performance Auditing." *Public Administration Review*, 34 (July–August 1974), 318–327.

Buchanan, Garth, Pamela Horst, and John Scanlon. "Improving Federal Evaluation Planning." *Evaluation*, 1, No. 2 (1973), 86–90.

———, and Joseph Wholey. "Federal Level Evaluation." *Evaluation*, 1, No. 1 (1972), 17–22.

Burton, Thomas L., and Gordon E. Cherry. *Social Research Techniques for Planners*. London: Allen and Unwin, 1970.

Campbell, Angus, Philip E. Converse, and Willard L. Rodgers. *The Quality of American Life: Perceptions, Evaluations, and Satisfactions*. New York: Russell Sage Foundation, 1976.

Campbell, Donald T. "Considering the Case Against Experimental Evaluations of Social Innovations." *Administrative Science Quarterly*, 15 (March 1970), 110–113.

———. "Reforms as Experiments." *American Psychologist*, 24 (April 1969), 409–429.

———, and Donald W. Fiske. "Convergent and Discriminant Validation by the Multitrait-Multimethod Matrix." *Psychological Bulletin*, 56 (March 1959), 81–105.

———, and H. Laurence Ross. "The Connecticut Crackdown on Speeding: Time-Series Data in Quasi-Experimental Analysis." *Law and Society Review*, 3 (August 1968), 33–54.

———, and Julian C. Stanley. *Experimental and Quasi-Experimental Designs for Research*. Chicago: Rand McNally, 1966.

Caporaso, James A., and Leslie L. Roos, Jr. (eds.). *Quasi-Experimental Approaches: Testing Theory and Evaluating Policy*. Evanston, Ill.: Northwestern University Press, 1973.

Caro, Francis G. "Approaches to Evaluative Research: A Review." *Human Organization*, 28 (Summer 1969), 87–99.

———. "Issues in the Evaluation of Social Programs." *Review of Educational Research*, 41 (April 1971), 87–114.

——— (ed.). *Readings in Evaluation Research*. New York: Russell Sage Foundation, 1971.

Carter, Reginald. "Clients' Resistance to Negative Findings and the Latent Conservative Function of Evaluation Studies." *American Sociologist*, 6 (May 1971), 118–124.

Chatterjee, Pranab. "Decision-Support System: A Case Study in Evaluative Research." *Journal of Applied Behavioral Science*, 11 (January–February–March 1975), 62–74.

Cheremisinoff, Paul N. (ed.). *Industrial Pollution Control: Measurement and Instrumentation*. Westport, Conn.: Technomic, 1976.

Cho, Yong Hyo. "A Multiple Regression Model for the Measurement of the Public Policy Impact on Big City Crime." *Policy Sciences*, 3 (December 1972), 435–455.

Christ, Carl F. *Econometric Models and Methods*. New York: Wiley, 1966.

Cochran, William G., and Gertrude M. Cox. *Experimental Designs*. 2nd ed. New York: Wiley, 1957.

Cohen, David. "Politics and Research: Evaluation of Social Action Programs in Education." *Review of Educational Research*, 40 (April 1970), 213–238.

Cohen, Jacob. "Multiple Regression as a General Data-Analytic System." *Psychological Bulletin*, 70 (December 1968), 426–443.

Coleman, James S. *Policy Research in the Social Sciences*. Morristown, N.J.: General Learning Corp., 1972.

Cook, Thomas J., and Frank P. Scioli. *Methodologies for Analyzing Public Policies*. Lexington, Mass.: Lexington Books, 1975.

Cronbach, Lee J. "Beyond the Two Disciplines of Scientific Psychology." *American Psychologist*, 30 (February 1975), 116–127.

Davis, Howard R. "Four Ways to Goal Attainment: An Overview." *Evaluation*, 1, No. 2 (1973), 43–49.

Delbercq, Andre L., and Andrew H. Van de Ven. "A Group Process Model for Problem Identification and Program Planning." *Journal of Applied Behavorial Science*, 7 (July–August 1971), 466–492.

Deniston, O. Lynn, Irwin M. Rosenstock, and V. A. Getting. "Evaluation of Program Effectiveness." *Public Health Reports*, 83 (April 1968), 323–335.

————, Irwin M. Rosenstock, W. Welch, and V. A. Getting. "Evaluating Health Programs." *Public Health Reports*, 85 (September 1970), 835–840.

Dolbeare, Kenneth (ed.). *Public Policy Evaluation*. Beverly Hills, Calif.: Sage, 1975.

Donabedian, Avedis. "Evaluating the Quality of Medical Care." *Milbank Memorial Fund Quarterly*, 44 (July 1966), Part 2, 166–203.

Drucker, Peter F. "Managing the Public Service Institution." *Public Interest*, 30 (Fall 1973), 43–60.

Duncan, Otis Dudley. *Introduction to Structural Equation Models*. New York: Academic Press, 1975.

————. "Path Analysis: Sociological Examples." *American Journal of Sociology*, 72 (July 1966), 1–16.

Dunnette, Marvin D. (ed.). *Handbook of Industrial and Organizational Psychology*. Chicago: Rand McNally, 1975.

Dye, Thomas R. *Understanding Public Policy*. Englewood Cliffs, N.J.: Prentice-Hall, 1972.

Etzioni, Amitai. "Alternative Conceptions of Accountability." *Hospital Progress*, 55 (June 1974), 34–39.

————, and Edward W. Lehman. "Some Dangers in 'Valid' Social Measurement." *Annals of the American Academy of Political and Social Science*, 373 (September 1967), 1–15.

Eulau, Heinz, and Kenneth Prewitt. *Labyrinths of Democracy: Adaptations,*

Linkages, Representation, and Policies in Urban Politics. Indianapolis: Bobbs-Merrill, 1973.

Evan, William M. (ed.). *Organizational Experiments: Laboratory and Field Research.* New York: Harper & Row, 1971.

Evans, John W. "Evaluating Social Action Programs." *Social Science Quarterly*, 50 (December 1969), 568–581.

Fairweather, George W. *Methods for Experimental Social Innovation.* New York: Wiley, 1967.

Fanshel, S., and J. W. Bush. "A Health Status Index and Its Applications to Health Services Outcomes." *Operations Research*, 18 (November–December 1970), 1021–1066.

Federal Statistics: Report of the President's Commission. Vol. II. Washington, D.C.: U.S. Government Printing Office, 1971.

Ferman, Louis A. (ed.). "Evaluating the War on Poverty." *Annals of the American Academy of Political and Social Science*, 385 (September 1969), entire issue.

Finsterbusch, Kurt, and C. P. Wolf (eds.). *Methodology of Social Impact Assessment.* Stroudsburg, Pa.: Dowden, Hutchinson and Ross, 1977.

Fox, Karl A. *Econometric Analysis for Public Policy.* Ames: Iowa State University Press, 1958.

———. *Social Indicators and Social Theory.* New York: Wiley, 1974.

Frank, Charles R., Jr. *Statistics and Econometrics.* New York: Holt, Rinehart & Winston, 1971.

Franklin, Jack L., and Jean H. Thrasher. *An Introduction to Program Evaluation.* New York: Wiley-Interscience, 1976.

Freeman, Howard E., and Clarence C. Sherwood. *Social Research and Social Policy.* Englewood Cliffs, N.J.: Prentice-Hall, 1970.

Gass, Saul I., and Roger L. Sisson. *A Guide to Models in Governmental Planning and Operations.* Potomac, Md.: Sanger Books, 1975.

Gilbert, John P., and Frederick Mosteller. "The Urgent Need for Experimentation." In Frederick Mosteller and Daniel P. Moynihan (eds.), *On Equality of Educational Opportunity.* New York: Random House, 1972.

Glaser, Daniel. *Routinizing Evaluation: Getting Feedback on Effectiveness of Crime and Delinquency Programs.* Washington, D.C.: Center for Studies of Crime and Delinquency, National Institute of Mental Health, 1974.

Glaser, Edward M., and Thomas Backer. "A Clinical Approach to Program Evaluation." *Evaluation*, 1, No. 3 (1973), 46–49.

Glass, Gene V. "Analysis of Data on the Connecticut Speeding Crackdown as a Time-Series Quasi-Experiment." *Law and Society Review*, 3 (August 1968), 55–76.

——— (ed.). *Evaluation Studies: Review Annual*, I. Beverly Hills, Calif.: Sage, 1976.

———, Victor L. Willson, and John M. Gottman. *Design and Analysis of*

Time-Series Experiments. Boulder: Colorado Associated University Press, 1975.

Glennan, Thomas K., Jr. *Evaluating Federal Manpower Programs: Notes and Observations.* Santa Monica, Calif.: Rand Corp., September 1969.

Goldberger, Arthur S., and Otis Dudley Duncan (eds.). *Structural Equation Models in the Social Sciences.* New York: Seminar Press, 1973.

Gordon, Robert A. "Issues in Multiple Regression." *American Journal of Sociology,* 73 (March 1968), 592–616.

Granger, Robert L., et al. *The Impact of Head Start: An Evaluation of the Effects of Head Start on Children's Cognitive and Affective Development.* Vol. I. Report to the Office of Economic Opportunity by Westinghouse Learning Corporation and Ohio University, June 1969.

Greenberger, Martin, Mathew A. Crenson, and Brian L. Crissey. *Models in the Policy Process.* New York: Russell Sage Foundation, 1976.

Griliches, Zvi (ed.). *Price Indexes and Quality Change: Studies in New Methods of Measurement.* Cambridge, Mass.: Harvard University Press, 1971.

Gronlund, Norman (ed.). *Readings in Measurement and Evaluation.* New York: Macmillan, 1968.

Guttentag, Marcia. "Evaluation of Social Intervention Programs." *Annals of the New York Academy of Sciences,* 218 (June 1973), 3–13.

———. "Models and Methods in Evaluation Research." *Journal of the Theory of Social Behavior,* 1 (April 1971), 75–95.

——— (ed.). *Evaluation Studies: Review Annual,* II. Beverly Hills, Calif.: Sage, 1977.

Guttman, Louis. "Social Problem Indicators." *Annals of the American Academy of Political and Social Science,* 393 (January 1971), 40–46.

Habenstein, Robert W. (ed.). *Pathways to Data: Field Methods for Studying Ongoing Social Organizations.* Chicago: Aldine, 1970.

Hannan, Michael T. *Aggregation and Disaggregation in Sociology.* Lexington, Mass.: Lexington Books, 1971.

Hargrove, Erwin C. *The Missing Link: The Study of Implementation of Social Policy.* Washington, D.C.: Urban Institute, 1975.

Hatry, Harry, Richard E. Winnie, and Donald M. Fish. *Practical Program Evaluation for State and Local Government Officials.* Washington, D.C.: Urban Institute, 1973.

Hauser, Philip M. *Social Statistics in Use.* New York: Russell Sage Foundation, 1975.

Haveman, Robert H., and Julius Margolis (eds.). *Public Expenditure and Policy Analysis.* 2nd ed. Chicago: Rand McNally, 1977.

Hawkes, Roland K. "The Multivariate Analysis of Ordinal Measures." *American Journal of Sociology,* 76 (March 1971), 908–926.

Hawkins, Brett W. *Politics and Urban Policy.* Indianapolis: Bobbs-Merrill, 1971.

———, and Robert M. Stein. "Regional Planning Assistance: Its Distribution to Local Governments and Relationship to Local Grant Getting." *Journal of the American Institute of Planning*, 43 (July 1977), 279–288.

Heise, David R. *Causal Analysis*. New York: Wiley-Interscience, 1975.

Hellmuth, Jerome (ed.). *Compensatory Education: A National Debate*. Vol. III of *The Disadvantaged Child*. New York: Brunner/Mazel, 1970.

Henriot, Peter. *Political Aspects of Social Indicators: Implications for Research*. New York: Russell Sage Foundation, 1972.

Hersen, Michael, and David H. Barlow. *Single Case Experimental Designs*. New York: Pergamon, 1976.

Hetherington, Robert, et al. "The Nature of Program Evaluation in Mental Health." *Evaluation*, 2, No. 2 (1974), 78–82.

Hilton, Gordon. *Intermediate Politometrics*. New York: Columbia University Press, 1976.

Hinrichs, Harley H., and Graeme M. Taylor. *Systematic Analysis: A Primer on Benefit-Cost Analysis and Program Evaluation*. Pacific Palisades, Calif.: Goodyear, 1972.

Hochstim, Joseph R. "A Critical Comparison of Three Strategies of Collecting Data from Households." *Journal of the American Statistical Association*, 62 (September 1967), 976–989.

Holzer, Marc (ed.). *Productivity in Public Organizations*. Port Washington, N.Y.: Kennikat, 1976.

Hood, William C., and Tjalling C. Koopmans (eds.). *Studies in Econometric Method*. New York: Wiley, 1953.

Horst, Pamela, et al. "Program Management and the Federal Evaluator." *Public Administration Review*, 34 (July–August 1974), 300–308.

House, Peter W., and John McLeod. *Large-Scale Models for Policy Evaluation*. New York: Wiley-Interscience, 1977.

Hyman, Herbert H., Charles R. Wright, and Terence K. Hopkins. *Applications of Methods of Evaluation: Four Studies of the Encampment for Citizenship*. Los Angeles: University of California Press, 1962.

Jones, Charles O. *An Introduction to the Study of Public Policy*. Belmont, Calif.: Wadsworth, 1970.

Jones, E. Terrence. "Evaluating Everyday Policies: Police Activity and Crime Incidence." *Urban Affairs Quarterly*, 8 (March 1973), 267–279.

Kassebaum, Gene, David Word, and Daniel Wilner. *Prison Treatment and Parole Survival: An Empirical Assessment*. New York: Wiley, 1971.

Katz, Jay, Alexander M. Capron, and Eleanor S. Glass. *Experimentation with Human Beings*. New York: Russell Sage Foundation, 1972.

Kershaw, David N. "A Negative-Income-Tax Experiment." *Scientific American*, 227 (October 1972), 19–25.

Kiresuk, Thomas J., and Sander H. Lund. "Program Evaluation and the Management of Organizations." In Wayne F. Anderson, Bernard J. Frieden, and Michael J. Murphy (eds.), *Managing Human Services*. Washington, D.C.: International City Management Association, 1977, pp. 280–317.

Kirk, Roger E. *Experimental Design: Procedures for the Behavioral Sciences.* Belmont, Calif.: Brooks/Cole, 1968.

Kish, Leslie. "Some Statistical Problems in Research Design." *American Sociological Review,* 24 (June 1959), 328–338.

————. *Survey Sampling.* New York: Wiley, 1965.

Kitsuse, John J., and Aaron V. Ciccourel. "A Note on the Uses of Official Statistics." *Social Problems,* 11 (Fall 1963), 131–139.

Kmenta, Jan. *Elements of Econometrics.* New York: Macmillan, 1971.

Land, Kenneth C., and Seymour Spilerman (eds.). *Social Indicator Models.* New York: Russell Sage Foundation, 1975.

Laska, Eugene, et al. "The Multi-State Information System." *Evaluation,* 1, No. 1 (1972), 66–71.

Lasswell, Harold D. *A Pre-View of Policy Sciences.* New York: Elsevier, 1971.

Lave, Charles A., and James G. March. *An Introduction to Models in the Social Sciences.* New York: Harper & Row, 1975.

Lazarsfeld, Paul F., William H. Sewell, and Harold L. Wilensky. *The Uses of Sociology.* New York: Basic Books, 1967.

Lehne, Richard, and Donald W. Fiske. "The Impact of Urban Policy Analysis." *Urban Affairs Quarterly,* 10 (December 1974), 115–138.

Lempert, Richard. "Strategies of Research Design in the Legal Impact Study." *Law and Society Review,* 1 (November 1966), 111–132.

Lerman, Paul. "Evaluative Studies for Delinquents: Implications for Research and Social Policy." *Social Work,* 13 (July 1968), 55–64.

Levine, Robert A. *Public Planning: Failure and Redirection.* New York: Basic Books, 1972.

Levitan, Sar A. "Facts, Fancies, and Freeloaders in Evaluating Antipoverty Programs." *Poverty and Human Resources Abstract,* 4, No. 6 (1969), 13–16.

Lewis, Frank L., and Frank G. Zarb. "Federal Program Evaluation from the OMB Perspective." *Public Administration Review,* 34 (July–August 1974), 308–317.

Light, Richard J., and Paul V. Smith. "Choosing a Future: Strategies for Designing and Evaluating New Programs." *Harvard Educational Review,* 40 (Winter 1970), 1–28.

Lindblom, Charles E. *The Intelligence of Democracy.* New York: Free Press, 1965.

————. *The Policy-Making Process.* Englewood Cliffs, N.J.: Prentice-Hall, 1968.

Lord, Frederic M. "Statistical Adjustments when Comparing Preexisting Groups." *Psychological Bulletin,* 72 (November 1969), 336–337.

Lynn, Lawrence E., Jr. "A Federal Evaluation Office." *Evaluation,* 1, No. 2 (1973), 56–59.

Lyons, Gene M. (ed.). *Social Research and Public Policies.* Public Affairs Center, Dartmouth College, Hanover, N.H.: University Press of New England, 1975.

McDill, Edward L., Mary McDill, and J. Timothy Sprehe. *Strategies for*

Success in Compensatory Education: An Appraisal of Evaluation Research. Baltimore: Johns Hopkins Press, 1969.

MacRae, Duncan, Jr. "Policy Analysis as an Applied Social Science Discipline." *Administration and Society,* 6 (February 1975), 363–388.

Main, Earl D. "A Nationwide Evaluation of M. D. T. A. Institutional Job Training." *Journal of Human Resources,* 3 (Spring 1968), 159–170.

Marvin, Keith E., and James L. Hedrick. "GAO Helps Congress Evaluate Programs." *Public Administration Review,* 34 (July–August 1974), 327–333.

Mason, Robert, and Albert N. Halter. "The Application of a System of Simultaneous Equations to an Innovation Diffusion Model." *Social Forces,* 47 (December 1968), 182–195.

Mendenhall, William. *Introduction to Linear Models and the Design and Analysis of Experiments.* Belmont, Calif.: Wadsworth, 1968.

Merril, William C., and Karl A. Fox. *Introduction to Economic Statistics.* New York: Wiley, 1970.

Miller, Delbert C. *Handbook of Research Design and Social Measurement.* 3rd ed. New York: McKay, 1977.

Mohr, Lawrence B. "The Concept of Organizational Goal." *American Political Science Review,* 58 (June 1973), 470–471.

Mondale, Walter F. "Social Accounting, Evaluation, and the Future of the Human Sciences." *Evaluation,* 1, No. 1 (1972), 29–34.

Morehouse, Thomas A. "Program Evaluation: Social Research Versus Public Policy." *Public Administration Review,* 32 (November–December 1972), 868–874.

Mosteller, Frederick, and Daniel P. Moynihan (eds.). *On Equality of Educational Opportunity.* New York: Random House, 1972.

Moursund, Janet P. *Evaluation: An Introduction to Research Design.* Monterey, Calif.: Brooks/Cole, 1973.

Nachmias, David, and Chava Nachmias. *Research Methods in the Social Sciences.* New York: St. Martin's, 1976.

Namboodiri, N. Krishnan, Lewis F. Carter, and Hubert M. Blalock, Jr. *Applied Multivariate Analysis and Experimental Designs.* New York: McGraw-Hill, 1975.

Olson, Mancur, Jr. "An Analytical Framework for Social Reporting and Policy Analysis." *Annals of the American Academy of Political and Social Science,* 388 (March 1970), 112–126.

Oppenheim, Abraham N. *Questionnaire Design and Attitude Measurement.* New York: Basic Books, 1966.

Otis, Todd. "Measuring 'Quality of Life' in Urban Areas." *Evaluation,* 1, No. 1 (1972), 35–38.

Poland, Orville. "Program Evaluation and Administrative Theory." *Public Administration Review,* 34 (July–August 1974), 333–338.

President's Panel on Social Indicators. *Toward a Social Report.* Washington, D.C.: U.S. Government Printing Office, 1969.

Pressman, Jeffrey L., and Aaron Wildavsky. *Implementation: How Great*

Expectations in Washington Are Dashed in Oakland, or, Why It's Amazing that Federal Programs Work at All. Berkeley: University of California Press, 1973.

Quade, E. S. *Analysis for Public Decisions.* New York: Elsevier, 1975.

Reeder, Leo G., Linda Ramacher, and Sally Gorelnik. *Handbook of Scales and Indices of Health Behavior.* Pacific Palisades, Calif.: Goodyear, 1976.

Riecken, Henry W., and Robert F. Boruch (eds.). *Social Experimentation: A Method for Planning and Evaluating Social Intervention.* New York: Academic Press, 1974.

Rivlin, Alice M. *Systematic Thinking for Social Action.* Washington, D.C.: Brookings Institution, 1971.

Robinson, John P., Jerrold G. Rusk, and Kendra B. Head. *Measures of Political Attitudes.* Ann Arbor: Survey Research Center, University of Michigan, 1968.

————, and Phillip R. Shaver. *Measures of Social Psychological Attitudes.* Ann Arbor: Survey Research Center, University of Michigan, 1969.

Roos, Noralou. "Contrasting Social Experimentation with Retrospective Evaluation: A Health Care Perspective." *Public Policy,* 23 (Spring 1975), 241–257.

Rosenberg, Morris. *The Logic of Survey Analysis.* New York: Basic Books, 1968.

Ross, H. Laurence. "Law, Science, and Accidents: The British Road Safety Act of 1967." *Journal of Legal Studies,* 2 (January 1973), 1–78.

————, Donald T. Campbell, and Gene V. Glass. "Determining the Social Effects of a Legal Reform: The British 'Breathalyser' Crackdown of 1967." *American Behavioral Scientist,* 13 (March–April 1970), 493–509.

Rourke, Francis E. *Bureaucracy, Politics and Public Policy.* 2nd ed. Boston: Little, Brown, 1976.

Salasin, Susan. "Setting Program Priorities for People: Evaluating Environmental Programs." *Evaluation,* 1, No. 3 (1973), 14–16.

Scanlon, John W. *An Evaluation System to Support Planning Allocation and Control in a Decentralized, Comprehensive Manpower Program.* Washington, D.C.: Urban Institute, 1971.

Schulberg, Herbert, and Frank Baker. "Program Evaluation Models and the Implementation of Research Findings." *American Journal of Public Health,* 58 (July 1968), 1248–1255.

Schulberg, Herbert, Alan Sheldon, and Frank Baker (eds.). *Program Evaluation in the Health Fields.* New York: Behavioral Publications, 1970.

Sharkansky, Ira (ed.). *Policy Analysis in Political Science.* Chicago: Markham, 1970.

Shaver, Philip R., and Graham Staines. "Problems Facing Campbell's 'Experimental Society.' " *Urban Affairs Quarterly,* 7 (December 1971), 173–186.

Sjogren, Douglas D. "Measurement Techniques in Evaluation." *Review of Educational Research*, 40 (April 1970), 301–320.

Skogan, Wesley G. "The Validity of Official Crime Statistics." *Social Science Quarterly*, 55 (June 1974), 25–38.

Skutch, Margaret, and J. L. Schofer. "Goals-Delphis for Urban Planning: Concepts in Their Design." *Socio-Economic Planning Science*, 7 (June 1973), 305–313.

Staats, Elmer. "The Challenge of Evaluating Federal Social Programs." *Evaluation*, 1, No. 3 (1973), 50–54.

Starfield, Barbara. "Measurement of Outcome: A Proposed Scheme." *Milbank Memorial Fund Quarterly*, 52 (Winter 1974), 39–50.

Stein, Herman D., George M. Hougham, and Serapio R. Zalba. "Assessing Social Agency Effectiveness: A Goal Model." *Welfare in Review*, 6 (March–April 1968), 13–18.

Stogdill, Ralph M. (ed.). *The Process of Model-Building in the Behavioral Sciences*. Columbus: Ohio State University Press, 1970.

Stromsdorfer, Ernst W. "Determinants of Economic Success in Retraining the Unemployed: The West Virginia Experience." *Journal of Human Resources*, 3 (Spring 1968), 139–152.

Strotz, Robert H., and Herman O. Wold. "Recursive vs. Nonrecursive Systems: An Attempt at Synthesis." *Econometrica*, 28 (April 1960), 417–427.

Struening, Elmer L., and Marcia Guttentag (eds.). *Handbook of Evaluation Research*. 2 vols. Beverly Hills, Calif.: Sage, 1975.

Stufflebeam, Daniel L. "Toward a Science of Educational Evaluation." *Educational Technology*, 8 (July 30, 1968), 5–12.

Suchman, Edward A. *Evaluative Research*. New York: Russell Sage Foundation, 1967.

Summers, Gene F. *Attitude Measurement*. Chicago: Rand McNally, 1970.

Sundquist, James L. (ed.). *On Fighting Poverty*. New York: Basic Books, 1969.

Susser, Mervyn. *Causal Thinking in the Health Sciences: Concepts and Strategies of Epidemiology*. New York: Oxford University Press, 1973.

Tamur, Judith M., et al. (eds.). *Statistics: A Guide to the Unknown*. San Francisco: Holden-Day, 1972.

Thistlethwaite, Donald L., and Donald T. Campbell. "Regression-Discontinuity Analysis: An Alternative to the Ex Post Facto Experiment." *Journal of Educational Psychology*, 51 (December 1960), 309–317.

Thompson, Charles, and Gustav Rath. "The Administrative Experiment: A Special Case of Field Testing or Evaluation." *Human Factors*, 16 (June 1974), 238–252.

Tomkins, Richard. "Evaluating National Health Insurance Legislation: A Summary Review." *Hospital Administration*, 19 (Summer 1974), 74–84.

Tripodi, Tony, Irwin Epstein, and Carol Macmurray. "Dilemmas in Evaluation: Implications for Administrators of Social Action Programs." *American Journal of Orthopsychiatry*, 40 (October 1970), 850–857.

——, Phillip Fellin, and Irwin Epstein. *Social Program Evaluation: Guidelines for Health, Education and Welfare Administrators*. Itasca, Ill.: Peacock, 1971.

Tufte, Edward R. *Data Analysis for Politics and Policy*. Englewood Cliffs, N.J.: Prentice-Hall, 1974.

Tukey, John W. "Causation, Regression, and Path Analysis." In Oscar Kempthorne et al. (eds.), *Statistics and Mathematics in Biology*. Ames: Iowa State University Press, 1954.

U.S. Department of Health, Education, and Welfare. *Toward a Social Report*. Washington, D.C.: U.S. Government Printing Office, 1969.

——, Office of Education. *Preparing Evaluation Reports: A Guide for Authors*. Washington, D.C.: U.S. Government Printing Office, 1970.

Van Meter, Donald S., and Herbert B. Asher. "Causal Analysis: Its Promise for Policy Studies." *Public Policy Journal*, 2 (Winter 1973), 103–109.

Wade, Larry L. *The Elements of Public Policy*. Indianapolis: Bobbs-Merrill, 1971.

Walker, Robert A. "The Ninth Panacea: Program Evaluation." *Evaluation*, 1, No. 1 (1972), 45–53.

Waller, John, et al. *Monitoring for Criminal Justice Planning Agencies*. Washington, D.C.: Urban Institute, 1974.

Wardrop, James L. "Generalizability of Program Evaluation: The Danger of Limits." *Educational Product Report*, 2 (February 1969), 41–42.

Webb, Eugene J., et al. *Unobtrusive Measures: Nonreactive Research in the Social Sciences*. Chicago: Rand McNally, 1966.

Weisberg, Herbert I. *Short Term Cognitive Effects of Head Start Programs: A Report on the Third Year of Planned Variation—1971–1972*. Cambridge, Mass.: Huron Institute, 1973.

Weiss, Carol H. "Alternative Models of Program Evaluation." *Social Work*, 19 (November 1974), 675–681.

——. *Evaluation Research*. Englewood Cliffs, N.J.: Prentice-Hall, 1972.

—— (ed.). *Evaluating Action Programs: Readings in Social Action and Education*. Boston: Allyn and Bacon, 1972.

Weiss, Robert S., and Martin Rein. "Evaluation of Broad-Aim Programs: A Cautionary Case and a Moral." *Annals of the American Academy of Political and Social Science*, 385 (September 1969), 133–142.

Wholey, Joseph, and Bayla While. "Evaluation's Impact on Title I Elementary and Secondary Education Program Management." *Evaluation*, 1, No. 3 (1973), 73–76.

——, et al. *Federal Evaluation Policy*. 4th printing. Washington, D.C.: Urban Institute, 1975.

Wilcox, Leslie D., et al. (eds.), *Social Indicators and Societal Monitoring: An Annotated Bibliography*. San Francisco: Jossey-Bass, 1972.

Wilensky, Harold. *Organizational Intelligence: Knowledge and Policy in Government and Industry.* New York: Basic Books, 1967.

Wilkins, Leslie T. *Evaluation of Penal Measures.* New York: Random House, 1969.

Williams, Walter. "The Capacity of Social Science Organizations to Perform Large-Scale Evaluative Research." Public Policy Paper No. 2. Seattle: Institute of Governmental Research, University of Washington, 1971.

―――. *Social Policy Research and Analysis: The Experience in the Federal Social Agencies.* New York: Elsevier, 1971.

―――, and John W. Evans. "The Politics of Evaluation: The Case of Head Start." *Annals of the American Academy of Political and Social Science,* 385 (September 5, 1969), 118–132.

Wilner, Daniel, et al. "Data Bank and Program Evaluation." *Evaluation,* 3, No. 3 (1973), 3–6.

Wold, Herman O. "Econometrics as Pioneering in Nonexperimental Model Building." *Econometrica,* 37 (July 1969), 369–381.

Wolman, Harold. *Politics of Federal Housing.* New York: Dodd, Mead, 1971.

Wonnacott, Ronald J., and Wonnacott, Thomas H. *Econometrics.* New York: Wiley, 1970.

Zeisel, Hans. "Reducing the Hazards of Human Experiments Through Modifications in Research Design." *Annals of the New York Academy of Sciences,* 169 (January 1970), 475–486.

Zimring, Franklin E. "Firearms and Federal Law: The Gun Control Act of 1968." *Journal of Legal Studies,* 4 (January 1975), 133–198.

Index

academic awards study, 66, 67 (illustrated)

acknowledged social goals, output descriptive indicators and, 80–81

Affirmative Action (program), 14

"Age Patterns in Medical Care, Illness and Disability" (National Center for Health Statistics), 81

aggregation method, of constructing index numbers, 97 (table), 98 (table), 99–100

analytic indicators, function of, 81

Angell, Robert C., 78

Aronson, Elliot, 35

association, as formal property operative with interval scales, 87

autocorrelation, in time-series analysis, 142, 143 (illustrated)

Bardach, Eugene, 5

baseline studies, social indicators obtained through replication of, 82–83

base selection, for index number construction, 95 (table), 96 (table), 97

Boruch, Robert F., 43, 68

Boston (Mass.), Control-Series design study of handgun homicides in, 63 (illustrated), 64 (illustrated), 65

Budget, Bureau of the, 48

Campbell, Donald T., 24, 31, 57, 59, 66, 67, 103

Carlsmith, J. Merrill, 35

causal inferences, establishing, 7–9

Census Bureau, 81

Chapin, F. Stuart, 24

classic experimental design, 21–29
  comparison in, 23
  external validity of, 28–29
  internal validity of, 24–28
  manipulation in, 23–24
  table, 22

CNJ reports (Crime in New Jersey reports), 95 (table), 96 (table)

coefficient of autocorrelation, 142

coefficient of curvilinear correlation, 128

coefficient of determination, in linear correlation, 118

coefficient of reproducibility (CR), 90–91

Coleman, James S., 83

combined quasi-experimental designs, 68–70, 71 (illustrated)
Community Action Program, 13–14, 48
commutation, as formal property operative with interval scales, 87
comparison in classic experimental design, 23
comprehensive evaluation, 5–6
Connecticut speeding crackdown
Control-Series design study of, 62, 63 (illustrated)
Time-Series design study of, 58 (illustrated), 59 (illustrated), 60
construct validity, 102–103
Consumer Price Index, 93–94
content validity, 101–102
Contrasted Groups design, 51–53, 54 (illustrated), 55 (illustrated)
control (internal validity), in classic experimental design, 24–28
controlled experimentation, 30 (table), 31 (table), 32–33, 34 (illustrated), 35
Control-Series designs, 62, 63 (illustrated), 64 (illustrated), 65–66
CR (coefficient of reproducibility), 90–91
crime-control policies, Sellin-Wolfgang Index to evaluate, 98–100
Crime in New Jersey reports (CNJ reports), 95 (table), 96 (table)
Crombach, Lee J., 102, 106
cumulative nature, of measurement scales, 88
Current Population Reports (Census Bureau), 81
curvilinear regression analysis, 124–128
calculations for, table, 125
cyclical variations, in time-series analysis, defined, 135–136

DAS (Detroit Area Study), 82–83
data
analysis and interpretation of, 18
collection of, 17–18
selection of, for index number construction, 95

social indicators based on available, 81–82
sources of, for measurement, 74–80
data banks, 79–80
decomposition, measuring variations by, 142
Delphi technique, 15
demand characteristics, in laboratory experiment, 36
demographic accounting, social indicators based on, 83
descriptive social indicators, defined, 80
Detroit Area Study (DAS), 92–93
disaggregation of social indicators, defined, 80*n*
discriminative power (DP) of the item, 92 (table), 93
distribution, standard normal, table, 173
distribution, *t*, table, 174
documents, as data sources, 78–79
DP (discriminative power) of the item, 92 (table), 93
Duncan, Otis Dudley, 82
Dye, Thomas R., 3

Economic Opportunity, Office of (OEO), 42, 48
Economic Opportunity Act, 13
EEO (Equal Employment Opportunity), 14
emerging societal goals, output descriptive indicators and, 81
endogenous variables, defined, 156
Equal Employment Opportunity (EEO), 14
equation models. *See* nonrecursive models; recursive models; structural models
erratic variations, in time-series analysis, defined, 136
estimation, in nonrecursive models, 160 (illustrated), 161 (illustrated), 162–165, 166 (illustrated), 167–168
evaluation, 1–20
framework for, 6–9, 10 (illustrated), 11 (illustrated), 12

perspective on performance and, 1–6
evaluation research, 4–6
  defined, 4
  types of, 5–6
  stages of, 13–18
Executive Office of the President (EXOP), 2
exogenous variables, defined, 156
experimental mortality, as intrinsic factor, 26–27
experimental realism, 35–36
experimentation
  controlled, 30 (table), 31 (table), 32–33, 34 (illustrated), 35
  types of, 35–44
  See also classic experimental design
experimenter bias, 36–37
external validity, *See* generalizability
extrinsic factors, internal validity of classic experimental design and, 24–25

factorial designs, in controlled experimentation, 32–33, 34 (illustrated), 35
Federal Bureau of Investigation (FBI), 79
Federal Gun Control Act (1968), 62, 65
field experimentation, 38–39, 40 (table), 41–44
field observation, 78
Fisher, Ronald A., 32
Fiske, Donald W., 103
fixed-alternative questions, 76–77
focused interviews, 75
Freeman, Howard E., 5, 12

generalizability (external validity)
  of classic experimental design, 28–29
  reliability and, 106–107
Gilbert, John P., 43
Gleser, Goldine C., 106
goals
  acknowledged social, 80–81
  emerging societal, 81

identification of, as stage of evaluation research, 13–15
measurement of, 17
Gorham, William, 1
Guttman, Louis, 89
Guttman scaling (Guttman scalogram analysis), 89, 90 (tables), 91 (table)

Halter, Albert N., 164, 168
handgun homicides, Control-Series design study of, 62, 63 (illustrated), 64 (illustrated), 65
Head Start, 13, 48, 50, 68, 100
Head Start Planned Variation Study (HSPV study), 55–56
Health, Education and Welfare, Department of (HEW), 80
"Health Characteristics of Low-Income Persons" (National Center for Health Statistics), 81
historical factors, as intrinsic factors, 25
homicides, Control-Series design study of, 62, 63 (illustrated), 64 (illustrated), 65
Horst, Pamela, 6
Housing and Urban Development, Department of (HUD), 2
Hovland, Carl I., 38
HSPV study (Head Start Planned Variation Study), 55–56

identification
  estimation and exact, in nonrecursive models, 161–165, 166 (illustrated), 167–168
  in nonrecursive models, 157–160
  overidentification, in nonrecursive models, 168
  underidentification, in nonrecursive models, 161 (illustrated), 162 (illustrated)
impact evaluation, defined, 5
impact models, 9–12
  construction of, 15–16
  illustrated, 10, 11
impacts, outputs vs., 2–3
implementation, of field experiments, 41–44

index number, construction of, 93–94, 95–98 (tables), 99–100
indices, seasonal, 139, 140 (table), 141 (table)
inferences, establishing causal, 7–9
instrument decay, as intrinsic factor, 26
internal validity (control), as feature of classic experimental design, 24–28
interval scales, 87–88
interviews, 75–76
intrinsic factors, internal validity of classic experimental design and, 25–27

Johnson, Lyndon B., 5, 48

Kershaw, David N., 42

laboratory experimentation, 35–38
laboratory observation, 78
Lana, Robert E., 31
leading questions, 77
least-squares method
  in curvilinear regression, 126
  in linear regression, 114, 115 (illustrated), 116, 117 (illustrated), 118
  in mulitple regression, table, 131
  two-stage, 162, 163, 165, 167, 168
Light, Richard J., 43
Likert scales (technique of summated rating), 91, 92 (table), 93
linear correlation, 118, 119 (illustrated), 120, 121 (table), 122 (illustrated), 123
linear regression analysis, 112–124
  illustrated, 112, 113
  least-squares method in, 114, 115 (illustrated), 116, 117 (illustrated), 118
  linear correlation in, 118, 119 (illustrated), 120, 121 (table), 122 (illustrated), 123
long-term trends, 135–139
  linear, in time-series analysis, 136–137, 138 (table), 139
  in time-series analysis, defined, 135

Manhattan Bail Project, 22–23
manipulation, in classic experimental design, 23–24
Mason, Robert, 164, 168
maturation, 25–27
measurement
  construction of measures, 88–89, 90–92 (tables), 93–94, 95–98 (tables), 99–100
  of goals and variables, 17
  measurement scales, 84–88
  reliability of, 103–107
  with social indicators, 80–84
  sources of data for, 74–80
  validity of, 100–103
measurement artifacts, used in laboratory experimentation, 37–38
Meehl, Paul E., 102
Michigan, University of, 82
mortality, experimental, 26–27
Mosteller, Frederick, 43
multicollinearity problem, 134
multidimensional scaling, 93
multiple regression analysis, 18, 129–134
  illustrated, 129
  multicollinearity problem and, 134
  Performance Indicators in Education as application of, 133–134
  table, 131
mundane realism, defined, 35

National Center for Health Statistics, 81
National Library of Medicine, 79
Neighborhood Youth Corps, 68
New Jersey Negative Income Tax Experiment, 38–39, 40 (table), 41, 42, 66, 68
New Towns In-Town, 5
New York City, Control-Series design study of handgun homicides in, 63 (illustrated), 64 (illustrated), 65
New York Probation Department, 23
New York University, 22
nominal scales, 85–86

nondirective interviews, 75–76
nonlinear regression analysis, 18
nonrecursive models, 156–168
  defined, 157
  estimation in, 160 (illustrated),
    161 (illustrated), 162–165, 166
    (illustrated), 167–168
  identification in. *See* identification
normal distribution, standard, table,
  173
normal equations, of bivariate
  regression, 115

objective dimensions of life, defined,
  83
observation, 78
OEO (Office of Economic Opportunity), 42, 48
open-ended questions, 77
ordinal scales, 86–87
output descriptive social indicators,
  80–81
outputs, impacts vs., 2–3
overidentification, in nonrecursive
  models, 168

parallel forms methods, of determining reliability, 105
Park, Robert, 81
path coefficients, 148
performance, perspective on, 1–6
Performance Indicators in Education, 133–134
Planned Variation designs, 55–57
Postprogram-Only   Comparison
  Group design, 31 (illustrated),
  32
postprogram scores, in classic experimental design, 22
potential for change, output descriptive indicators and, 81
prediction bands, 117 (illustrated),
  122 (illustrated)
predictive validity, of measurement,
  100–101
pre-experimental designs, 47–51
preprogram scores, in classic experimental design, 22
process evaluation, defined, 5

product-moment coefficient in linear correlation, 120
purpose, definition of, in index
  number construction, 94

Quade, E. S., 9
quality of life, subjective and objective measures of, 83–84
quasi-experimental designs, 51–71
  combined, 68–70, 71 (illustrated)
  Constrasted Group designs as,
    51–53, 54 (illustrated), 55 (illustrated)
  Control-Series designs as, 62, 63
    (illustrated),   64   (illustrated),
    65–66
  Planned Variations designs as,
    55–57
  Regression-Discontinuity designs
    as, 66, 67 (illustrated), 68
  Time-Series design as, 57, 58–61
    (illustrated)
quasi-experimental evaluations with
  pre-experimental designs, 47–
  51
  See also quasi-experimental designs
Questionnaires, 76–78

Rajaratnam, Nageswari, 106
randomization
  in classic experimental design,
    27–28
  tie-breaking, 66, 67 (illustrated)
randomized experiments, at selected
  intervals, Regression-Discontinuity designs with, 70, 71 (illustrated)
rank values, defined, 86
reactive arrangements, generalizability of classical experimental
  design by, 29
realism, mundane and experimental, 35–36
recognition artifacts, as intrinsic factor, 26
recursive models, 146–156
  illustrated, 147
  path analysis of, 148, 149 (illustrated),   150,   151–153   (illus-

trated), 154, 155 (illustrated), 156

reduced form, of nonrecursive models of equation system, 164

reduced-form coefficients, 164

regression analysis
nonlinear, 18
residual terms in, 123–124
See also curvilinear regression analysis; linear regression analysis; multiple regression analysis; time-series analysis

regression coefficient, 112

Regression-Discontinuity designs, 66, 67 (illustrated), 68
with randomized experiments at selected intervals, 70, 71 (illustrated)

regression line, 115

reliability, of measurement, 103–107

Research, Plans, Programs and Evaluations, Office of (RPP&E), 49

research design, aim of, 16–17

residual path coefficient, 154

residual variance, 116

residual terms, in regression analysis, 123–124

residuals
defined, 114
geometrical interpretation of, illustrated, 115

Riecken, Henry, W., 43

riot-severity scale, table, 91

Rosenbloom, David H., 14

Rosenthal, Robert, 36

Rossi, Peter H., 25

RPP&E (Office of Research, Plans, Programs and Evaluations), 48

Salk vaccine study, 68–70

sample, representativeness of, and external validity of classic experimental design, 28–29

scattergrams
curvilinear regression, illustrated, 126
linear regression, 113 (illustrated), 122 (illustrated)

schedule-structured interviews, 75

seasonal indices, in short-term time-series analysis, 139, 140 (table), 141 (table)

seasonal variations, in time-series analysis, defined, 135

selection-maturation interaction, as intrinsic factor, 27

Sellin, Thorsten, 99

Sellin and Wolfgang Index of Delinquency, 98–100

Sherwood, Clarence C., 12

Sheldon, Eleanor B., 81

short-term time-series analysis, 139, 140 (table), 141 (table), 142

Siegel, Sidney, 84

Simon, Herbert, 7

simple aggregates, in construction of index numbers, 97 (table), 98

simple linear regression analysis, 18

simultaneous equation system, defined, 146

social accounting, social indicators based on, 83

social goals, output descriptive indicators and acknowledged, 80–81

social indicators, 80–84

societal goals, output descriptive indicators and emerging, 81

Solomon Four-Group design, 30 (illustrated), 31

split-half technique, to estimate reliability, 105–106

standardization, of goals, 17

standard normal distribution, table, 173

Stanley, Julian C., 24, 31, 57

Stone, Richard, 83

structural equation systems, defined, 145

structural models, 145–146

subjective measures, of quality of life, social indicators based on, 83–84

substitution, as formal property operative with interval scales, 87

summated rating, technique of (Likert scale), 91, 92 (table), 93 symmetry, as formal property operative with interval scales, 87

t distribution, table, 174
testing, as intrinsic factor, 26
test-retest technique, of reliability, 104–105
Thistlewaite, Donald L., 66
tie-breaking randomization, 66, 67 (illustrated)
time-series analysis, 134–143
   autocorrelation in, 142, 143 (illustrated)
   illustrated, 135
   linear long-term trends in, 136–137, 138 (table), 139
   measuring variations by decomposition in, 142
   short-term, 139, 140 (table), 141 (table), 142
Time-Series designs, 57, 58–61 (illustrated)
Tompkins, Gary L. 154
Toward a Social Report (HEW), 81
Toward Social Reporting: Next Steps (Duncan), 81
two-stage least-squares technique (2SLS), in nonrecursive models, 162, 163, 165, 167, 168

underidentification, in nonrecursive models, 161 (illustrated), 162 (illustrated)
uniqueness, as formal property operative with interval scales, 87

validity
   external. *See* Generalizability
   of field experiments, 41
   internal, 24–28
   of measurements, 100–103
variables
   exogenous and endogenous, 156
   measurement of, 17
Vera Institute, 22

Wanderer, Jules J., 91
weighted aggregates, in construction of index numbers, 98 (table), 99–100
Weisberg, Herbert I., 56
welfare expenditures, path analysis of, illustrated, 155
Weiss, Carol H., 4–5
Westinghouse study, 13
Wolfgang, Marvin E., 99

Zimring, Franklin E., 62